North Eastern Railway Branc[h

Lesser Railways Around Darlington
Fighting Cocks, Croft Depot, Forcett and Merrybent Branches

Robin B Coulthard and John G Teasdale,
with co-authors John P McCrickard and Richard V Webster

NORTH EASTERN RAILWAY ASSOCIATION

Contents

ISBN 978-1-911360-13-1
Typeset by John G Teasdale.
Printed in Great Britain by Amadeus Press, Ezra House, West 26 Industrial Estate, CLECKHEATON, BD19 4TQ.

THE NORTH EASTERN RAILWAY ASSOCIATION

Formed in 1961, the NERA caters for all those interested in the railways of north-east England, with particular focus on the North Eastern Railway, its constituents and successors, from their early history down to the present day. This also extends to the many industrial and smaller railways that operated alongside them. Interests range over all aspects of development, operation and infrastructure of the railway, including such diverse activities as locomotive history, rolling stock, train services, architecture, signalling, shipping, road vehicles and staff matters – both for the general enthusiast and model maker.

With in excess of 600 members, regular meetings are held in York, Darlington, Hull, and London. A programme of tours and walks is also arranged. The Association also holds an extensive archive of books, documents, photographs and drawings available for study by members and non-members alike.

Members receive a quarterly illustrated journal, the *North Eastern Express*, and a newsletter, covering membership topics, forthcoming meetings and events in the region. Over 200 issues of the *Express* have been published to date.

The Association also markets an extensive range of facsimiles of railway company documents, including diagram books, timetables and other booklets, while at the same time it is developing an expanding range of original publications, available to members at discounted prices.

For a membership prospectus, please contact :
   Membership Secretary, 7 Grenadier Drive, NORTHALLERTON, DL6 1SB.
   e-mail : membership@ner.org.uk
A list of NERA publications is available. Please send a Stamped Addressed 9" x 4" Envelope to :
   Publications Officer, 31 Moreton Avenue, Stretford, MANCHESTER, M32 8BP.

NERA Website : www.ner.org.uk

Front Cover Photograph : *On 27 April 1964, Ivatt 4MT Mogul No 43050 crosses the River Tees with the return portion of the Forcett pick-up goods. (JM Boyes / Armstrong Railway Photographic Trust)*

Title Page Photograph : *An unidentified Class A8 runs off the Fighting Cocks Branch on to the Darlington & Saltburn Branch at Oak Tree Junction with a diverted Darlington - Saltburn working. The signal boxes at Oak Tree and Geneva (Darlington) were of similar design and opened in 1887. (JW Armstrong / Armstrong Railway Photographic Trust)*

Introduction and Acknowledgements

Introduction

By 1825, waggonways were common in the north-east of England. They were used to convey coal from collieries to river-side staiths from which the coal was shipped onwards. On 27 September 1825 the Stockton & Darlington Railway (S&DR) was opened formally. Like the waggonways that had come before, the S&DR was primarily intended for the conveyance of coal; in the case of the S&DR, to staiths on the River Tees. However, unlike the waggonways, it would also be used to carry people and all manner of goods. A large measure of chaos attended the operation of traffic in the S&DR's early years, but lessons were learned – and applied all over the world.

The first branch to be described in this book, the Fighting Cocks Branch, began life as an integral part of the S&DR main line. That status was lost first when the S&DR was absorbed into the North Eastern Railway (NER) in 1863, and secondly when the NER diverted passenger traffic to a newly-constructed line in 1887.

The S&DR constructed branches off its main line, and one of these, the Croft Depot Branch, is described next. The final two lines to be covered in this book, the Forcett Railway and the Merrybent & Darlington Railway, both started life as independent undertakings; they were constructed by entrepreneurs mainly to exploit local deposits of limestone. In due course, both would be absorbed into the NER or its successor, the London & North Eastern Railway.

All four lines are long since closed to traffic.

Acknowledgements

This book, very much a collaborative effort, is based upon the regular photographic exhibitions that the North Eastern Railway Association (NERA) mounts at the Head of Steam Museum, Darlington, and upon articles published in the *North Eastern Express*.

The mounting of the exhibitions relevant to this book was the responsibility of Robin Coulthard, and he enjoyed the full support and assistance of the team working in the NERA's archive at McNay Street, Darlington. Core members of the team are: Richard Lacey (NERA Archivist); Tom Burnham; Les Cairnes; David Ramsden; Eddie Scarlett; Sam Woods. Robin Coulthard, and the McNay Street team, also benefit from the full support and assistance of the staff at the Head of Steam Museum, principally Leona White-Hannant, Museum Manager Curator, and Alison Grange, Collections & Learning Assistant.

The authors of articles in the *Express*, John Teasdale, John McCrickard and Richard Webster, benefited from extensive support from NERA members in the way of information, photographs, documents *etc.*, support which has continued into the production of this book: John Addyman; the late John Boyes; Pete Coombs; David Corfield (NERA Chairman); Michael Denholm; Nicholas Fleetwood; the late Ray Goad; Michael Grocock; the late Geoffrey Horsman; Neil Mackay; John Midcalf (also a trustee of the Armstrong Railway Photographic Trust); Chris Nettleton; Richard Pulleyn; Duncan Wilcock; David Williamson (NERA Publications Officer); Claire Williamson; the late Chris Woolstenholmes; Alan Young. We have also benefited from the generous assistance of members of the broader community of railway enthusiasts and public institutions: John Alsop; Richard Barber (Secretary, Armstrong Railway Photographic Trust); Dave Burdon; John and Edith Davison; Mandy Faye and Kathryn Williamson (Centre for Local Studies, Darlington Public Library); Trevor Horner; Chris Lloyd (Chief Features Writer, *The Northern Echo*); Cliff Shepherd (Editor, the *Industrial Railway Record*); Jim Shields; John Young; staff at The National Archives, Kew, and The National Railway Museum, York.

This book could not have been produced without you; the authors extend their heartfelt thanks.

A view looking south along the Merrybent & Darlington towards the bridge over the River Tees. Milepost 2 was erected by the North Eastern Railway following an instruction issued in March 1905 that all of the company's lines were to be re-measured and standard mileposts erected. The photograph was taken in the 1950s. (JW Armstrong / Armstrong Railway Photographic Trust)

Fighting Cocks Branch

The stretch of railway designated by the North Eastern Railway as the Fighting Cocks Branch was not a branch line as such, but had been constructed and opened as part of the Stockton & Darlington Railway's main line. As defined by the North Eastern, the western end of the Fighting Cocks Branch was at Albert Hill Junction. At the junction, a west to south curve (the Parkgate Loop) connected with the York & Newcastle Branch (*i.e.* the North Eastern's main line) north of Darlington. This curve had started off life as the northern end of the S&DR's Croft Depot Branch. From Albert Hill Junction, the Fighting Cocks Branch ran eastwards, crossing the main line on the level. The eastern end of the branch was at Oak Tree Junction, 4 miles 20.58 chains from Albert Hill Junction. This was where a line running eastwards from Darlington, opened on 1 July 1887, joined the former S&DR's main line. The 1887 line from Darlington, and most of the eastern portion of the former S&DR, was designated the North Eastern Railway's Darlington & Saltburn Branch.

Stockton & Darlington Railway

The origins of the S&DR are well known. Initially, there were proposals for a canal or a tramroad to convey coal from collieries located north-west of Darlington to the River Tees at Stockton. These proposals were eventually honed in favour of a tramroad or railway, and a route surveyed by George Overton was presented to Parliament. An Act was obtained on 19 April 1821, though the route as subsequently constructed as a railway would be improved upon by George Stephenson, who became the S&DR's engineer.(1)

The first sod for the construction of the S&DR was cut on 13 May 1822 at the Stockton end of the line (which was to be constructed to Overton's survey). The first rails, of malleable rather than cast-iron, were laid a few days later on 23 May. The fish-bellied rails were 12 or 15 feet long, 28 lb per yard. The main line was single-track. To allow traffic to pass, every quarter of a mile or so there was a turn-out or passing place. These loops of track off the main line were mostly laid with cheaper cast-iron rails (as was a small part of the main line). The rails sat in cast-iron chairs, which were pinned to sleeper blocks. George Stephenson thought that the rails would last more or less indefinitely, so wished to use stone rather than wood for the blocks. However, the nearest suitable quarry was north of Darlington. Transport of stone blocks by road to Stockton being prohibitive, the eastern end of the S&DR was laid using wooden blocks cut from old ships' timbers.

As to the gauge of the S&DR, this was also determined by Stephenson. He had successfully built steam locomotives to work on the Killingworth waggonway, which was laid to a gauge of 4 feet 8 inches. He used this gauge when he constructed the 8 mile long Hetton Colliery Railway, which was to be partly worked by his locomotives. If Stephenson got his way, at least some of the traffic over the S&DR would also be worked using locomotives. Having a lot on his mind at the time, he evidently did not give much thought as to whether the gauge appropriate for a colliery railway was also appropriate for a public railway that would convey traffic of a much more varied nature than coal. Though he surely cannot be faulted for not anticipating that some 90 years later, purely for aesthetic reasons, the designers of the North Eastern's Class Z express passenger locomotive would squeeze one connecting rod and three separate sets of valve gear between its frames… The S&DR was laid to a gauge of 4 feet 8 inches. With the addition of an extra half inch to allow freedom of lateral motion for coned wheels, this became the British standard gauge.

When Overton had laid out his route for the S&DR, in order to minimise earthworks he had tended to follow contour lines. However, this had resulted in a somewhat sinuous route and a long stretch where loaded coal trains being worked to Stockton would be faced with an uphill gradient. Stephenson did not ignore terrain when he made his own survey, but he did not let it dominate his thinking either. He surveyed a route comprising long straight stretches and very large radius curves. The gradient was in favour of loaded coal trains along the entire route. Constructing the necessary earthworks would be more expensive, but this would be compensated for by the fact that Stephenson's route was some 3 miles shorter than Overton's. The most radical difference between the two routes was in the area that would in the future comprise the Fighting Cocks Branch; indeed, the two routes crossed each other at more or less right angles.

Most of Stephenson's changes to Overton's route could not be accommodated within the limits of deviation allowed by the S&DR's 1821 Act. A new Act was obtained on 23 May 1823.(2) The 1823 Act also sanctioned the use of steam locomotives to convey goods, minerals and passengers. As the railway was intended to operate in the same way as did a turnpike road, locomotives could be used by the S&DR itself or by any person paying a toll and authorized by the railway company so to do.

There were no particular civil engineering challenges on the route of the Fighting Cocks Branch, though as all digging was by hand there was a huge amount of hard graft. There was, however, an issue where the railway crossed the Darlington to Stockton turnpike. The railway would cross the road on the level. In order to smooth the gradient for the railway, it was necessary to raise the road where it passed through a hollow. Despite the fact that the work would actually improve the road, two of the trustees of the turnpike objected. Of course, the real objection was that the railway would render the turnpike redundant. The trustees, in their capacity as local magistrates, fined the workmen who had raised the road. After further to and fro, the magistrates agreed with the S&DR's solicitors that the issue would be placed before a higher court. However, on 6 September 1824, the Commissioners of the Road collectively came to the conclusion that they were on a hiding to nothing, and abandoned the case.

Albert Hill Junction looking east, February 1968. This marked the commencement of the Fighting Cocks Branch following the opening of the alternative route to Dinsdale in 1887, though by the time the photograph was taken the branch had closed as a through route. The Fighting Cocks Branch runs straight ahead (the tracks are still in place here) whilst the Parkgate Loop bears right. Albert Hill signal box (left) controlled the junction; this box would itself close in September 1969 and be demolished the following August. Part of the municipal gas works is visible behind the signal box, and Thomas Summerson's Albert Hill Foundry is visible in the far background; both were served by sidings off the Fighting Cocks Branch. (RB Coulthard / NERA Collection RC134)

The S&DR opened formally on 27 September 1825. The main line was complete. However, Stephenson's estimates for the construction cost of the line had proved to be insufficient by far, and although work had started on some of the proposed branches none had been completed apart from the half-mile Darlington Depots Branch (which served a coal depot at Northgate). Initially, the S&DR Board took a very hands-off approach to the working of traffic over the railway. The conveyance of all traffic – goods, minerals and passengers – was contracted out. Even the driving of the S&DR's own locomotives was contracted out. At first, enginemen were paid fixed wages, but from 17 February 1826, the men were paid on a tonnage hauled basis; from the money received, the engineman had to pay their own wages, plus pay for coal, oil,

tallow *etc.* The combination of a significant number of independent contractors and both horse- and locomotive-drawn trains running over a single-track main line – albeit with passing places – proved to be a fine recipe for chaos. A measure of order was created when the main line from Brusselton Incline (north-west of Darlington) to Stockton was doubled, but the ultimate solution was for the S&DR to take the working of all traffic into its own hands. This process began in 1833 when the S&DR bought out the coach proprietors working passenger traffic over the railway, and henceforth ran its own passenger trains. (Except on a Sunday; passengers wishing to travel on a Sunday could, however, hire a coach from the S&DR and pay the required toll for its use on the railway.)

In due course, the S&DR was steadily upgraded, losing the primitive characteristics which had given it – to modern eyes at least – a lot of its charm. The early locomotives, with their thickets of connecting and valve gear rods above the boiler, were replaced by sleek machines with their valve gear discretely hidden between the frames. The track was upgraded, the fish-bellied rails and sleeper blocks being replaced by bull-headed rail and transverse wooden sleepers.

The S&DR steadily expanded too. However, the largest railway company in the north-east of England was the North Eastern. On 13 July 1863, the S&DR merged with the North Eastern, though it retained a large measure of independence as the North Eastern's Darlington Section until 1876. Until the early 20th Century, the former S&DR formed the core of North Eastern's Central Division.

First Class Train.
Aycliffe Lane
TO
FIGHTING COCKS
No.   Outside, 1ˢ 0ᵈ

day of   184

Please to hold this Ticket till called for.

A Stockton & Darlington Railway ticket, printed for issue in the 1840s. This type of ticket, which depended upon a clerk adding by hand details such as number of issue and date, would soon be replaced by fully-printed tickets as devised by Thomas Edmondson.

UP.

	1	2	3	4	5	6	7	8	9	10	11	12	13	14	15	16	17	18	19	SUNDAYS. 1	2	3
	GOODS.	GOODS.	PASSR.	GOODS.	GOODS.	PASSR.	PASSR.	PASSR.	GOODS.	PASSR.	GOODS.	PASSR.	PASSR.	GOODS.	GOODS.	PASSR.	PASSR.	PASSR.	PASSR.	PSSR.	PSSR.	
	a.m.	a.m.	a.m.	a.m.	a.m.	a.m.	a a.m.	a a.m.	b a.m.	a.m.	p.m.	p.m.	p.m.	p.m.	p.m.	p.m.	p.m.	p.m.	p.m	a.m.	p.m.	
SALTBURN ....dep.	...	...	...	...	...	8 30	10 10	...	10 15	11 20	...	1 40	...	...	...	4 0	...	5 30	6 25	...	5 25	...
Marske	...	...	...	...	...	8 35	10 15	...	10 25	11 25	...	1 45	...	...	...	4 5	...	5 35	6 30	...	5 30	...
REDCAR ....{ arr dep	...	...	...	...	...	8 45	10 23	...	10 45 11 10	11 35	...	1 55	...	...	...	4 15	...	5 50	6 40	...	5 40 5 45	...
Lazenby	...	...	...	...	...		10 28	...			...	2 3	...	...	...	4 25	...	6 0	6 50	...	5 50	...
Eston	...	...	...	...	...	8 55	10 33	...	11 25	11 45	...		...	...	3 30	4 30	...	6 5	...	...	5 55	...
Cleveland Port	...	...	...	...	...		10 37	...	11 35		1 0		...	...			...		...	...	...	...
MIDDLESBRO' ....{ arr dep	...	...	6 0	6 30	8 20	9 5	10 43	11 45	12 10 12 35	11 53	1 30 2 0	2 10	...	3 0	4 30	4 35	5 50	6 13	7 0	...	6 0	...
Newport	...	...	...	...			10 47	11 48		11 56			...	3 15			5 53		...	...	...	...
South Stockton	...	...	...	...	8 40				12 45				...	3 30			6 0		...	...	...	...
STOCKTON ......{ arr dep	...	...	6 10	...	9 20 10 0	9 15	10 52	11 53	1 0 1 10	12 3		2 18	...	4 30 4 50	5 0 5 20	4 45 4 55	6 23 6 38	7 10 7 18	...	6 10 6 20	...
Preston Junction	...	...	6 18	7 20	10 20	9 30	...		1 25	12 11	2 20	2 32	...						...		...	...
Yarm	...	...	...		10 30		...		1 35		2 30		...	5 0		5 7		6 53	...		6 30	...
Middleton and Dinsdale ..	...	...	...		10 50	9 42	...		1 55	12 25		2 45	...			5 15		7 0	7 40		6 40	...
DARLINGTON ....{ arr dep	5 0 5 30	6 0 6 20	6 40 6 45 6 55	8 0	11 10 11 30 11 50	9 50 10 30 10 40	...		2 15 2 30 2 50	12 53 12 35	3 15	3 0 3 10	4 15 4 25	5 40	6 5 7 30	5 15		7 10 7 20		7 30 7 40		...
Aycliffe and Heighington..	5 30	6 20	6 55		11 50	10 40	...		2 50			3 10	4 25					7 20		7 40		...
Simpasture	5 40	6 30	...	7 0	12 0		...		3 0													...
Shildon	6 0	7 0	7 3	7 40	12 15	10 50	...		3 15			3 20	4 35		8 0			7 30		7 50		...
Bishop Auckland	6 30	...	7 15	8 40	12 50	11 0	...		...			3 30	4 45		8 20			7 40		8 5		...
Etherley	7 0	...	7 25	9 20	1 20	11 10	...		...			3 40			8 40			7 48		8 15		...
Witton Junction	7 10	...	7 30	9 40	1 30	11 13	...		...			3 45			8 50			7 53		8 20		...
Beechburn	...	...					...		...									8 0				...
CROOK ....{ arr dep	7 40	...	7 45		1 50	11 25 11 30	...		...			4 0 5 15			9 20			8 5				...
Sunniside	8 0	...	...		2 10		...		...						9 40			...				...
Tow Law	9 30	...	...			12 0	...		...			5 40						...				...
Burn Hill Junction	...	...	...			12 15	...		...			5 55						...				...
Cold Rowley	...	...	...			12 25	...		...			6 5						...				...
CARRHOUSE	10 30	...	...			12 35	...		...			6 15						...				...

(a) Nos. 7 and 8 run on Wednesdays only.   (b) On Wednesdays No. 9 will take Cattle from Stockton.

DOWN.

	1	2	3	4	5	6	7	8	9	10	11	12	13	14	15	16	17	18	19	SUNDAYS. 1	2	3
	PASSR.	GOODS.	GOODS.	PASSR.	GOODS.	PASSR.	GOODS.	GOODS.	GOODS.	PASSR.	PASSR.	PASSR.	PASSR.	GOODS.	PASSR.	GOODS.	PASSR.	PASSR.	GOODS.	PSSR.	PSSR.	
	a.m.	a.m.	a.m.	a.m.	a.m.	a.m.	a.m.	a.m.	a.m.	a p.m.	p.m.	p.m.	b p.m.	p.m.	p.m.	p.m.	p.m.	p.m.	p.m.	a.m.	p.m.	
CARRHOUSE ....dep	...	...	...	...	...	8 5	9 30	...	...	...	...	...	...	...	...	4 0	...	...	...	...	...	...
Cold Rowley	...	...	...	...	...	8 10	...	...	...	...	...	...	...	...	...	4 10	...	...	...	...	...	...
Burn Hill Junction	...	...	...	...	...	8 20	...	...	...	...	...	...	...	...	...	4 20	...	...	...	...	...	...
Tow Law	...	...	...	...	...	8 35	10 30	...	...	...	...	...	...	...	...	4 35	...	...	...	...	...	...
Sunniside	...	...	...	...	...		...	9 0	...	...	...	...	...	3 30	...		...	...	9 50	...	...	...
CROOK ....{ arr dep	...	...	...	7 15	...	9 0 9 5	...	9 15	...	...	12 25	2 30 2 33	...	3 40	...	5 10 5 20 5 23	...	10 0	...	...	...	...
Beechburn	...	...	...	7 18	...		...		...	...			...		...		...		...	...	...	...
Witton Junction	...	...	...	7 30	...	9 13	...	9 45	...	...	12 33	2 40	...	3 50	...	5 32	...	10 30	...	...	5 30	...
Etherley and Witton Park	...	...	...	7 35	...	9 20	...	10 10	...	...	12 38	2 45	...	4 10	...	5 37	...	10 40	...	...	5 35	...
Bishop Auckland	...	...	...	7 45	...	9 30	...	10 40	...	...	12 50	3 0	2 55	4 35	...	5 50	...	11 0	...	...	5 55	...
Shildon	...	...	6 50	7 50	...	9 38	...	11 0	12 30	...	12 58	3 10	...	5 10	...	5 58	...	11 20	...	...	6 5	...
Simpasture	...	...	7 0		...		...	11 15	12 40	...			...	5 20	...		...		...	...		...
Aycliffe and Heighington..	...	...	7 10	8 0	...	9 50	...	11 30		...	1 10	3 20	...	5 30	6 8		...		...	...	5 15	...
DARLINGTON ....{ arr dep	6 0 6 7	6 10	8 0 8 15	8 35 8 42	9 5 9 25	10 20 10 28	...	12 0	1 10 1 45	...	1 20 1 45 1 53	3 35 3 55 4 5	...	5 50	6 18	6 45 6 53	8 30 8 38		12 0	7 0 7 10	6 25	...
Yarm		6 40	8 40				...	1 30	2 10	...			...						...			...
Preston Junction	6 20	6 50	8 45	8 55	9 30	10 38	...	1 40	2 15	...	2 5	4 20	...	5 0		7 5	8 50		...	7 20		...
STOCKTON ......{ arr dep	6 30	7 0	9 0 9 40	9 5	...	10 50	...	1 50		1 45	2 17	4 30	...		6 10	7 17	9 5		...	7 30		...
South Stockton		7 10	10 0		...		...	2 0		...			...	5 35	6 15		...		...	7 35		...
Newport	...			9 10	...		...			...	1 50		...		6 20		...		...			...
MIDDLESBRO' ....{ arr dep	6 40	7 30	10 10 11 0	9 16	9 55	11 0	...	2 15	2 50	1 55	2 27	4 40	...	5 50		7 28	9 15		...	7 40		...
Cleveland Port			11 20	9 19	...		...		3 0	...		4 45	...			7 33	...		...			...
Eston	6 47		11 40	9 23	...	11 7	...			...	2 34	4 50	...	6 10		7 38	...		...	7 50		...
Lazenby	...			9 26	...		...			...		4 58	...			7 40	...		...			...
REDCAR ....{ arr dep	7 0		12 0 12 20	9 35	...	11 25	...			...	2 55	5 0	...			7 52	...		...	8 0		...
Marske	7 5		12 45	9 40	...	11 30	...			...	3 0	5 6	...			7 57	...		...	8 5		...
SALTBURN	7 15		1 0	9 50	...	11 35	...			...	3 10	5 15	...			8 5	...		...	8 25		...

(a) No. 10 runs on Wednesdays only.   (b) No. 13 runs on Saturdays only.

The North Eastern Railway had become the largest railway company in the north-east of England by a combination of take-overs of other companies and by constructing new branch lines. In the mid 1880s, serious thought was given to a new branch line running eastwards from Darlington. The S&DR had been constructed primarily as a railway to convey coal to Stockton. There had been no need, therefore, for the railway to pass close to Darlington. The S&DR's passenger station serving the town was well to the north of the town centre; the 1842 station, replacing an earlier one, was named Darlington (North Road). There was a

Previous page : This extract, detailing passenger and goods trains on the former S&DR main line, is from the North Eastern Railway's Working Time Table in effect from April 1864. (Mineral trains are not included in the timetable.) As it pertains to the future Fighting Cocks Branch, the station of interest is Middleton and Dinsdale (which would in due course be re-named Fighting Cocks). In the Down direction (eastbound trains) the station is served on weekdays by seven passenger trains and one goods, the 6:50 am Shildon - Saltburn (and one passenger train on Sundays). In the Up direction there are only five passenger trains, but two goods, the 8:20 am Middlesbrough - Sunniside and the 10:15 am Saltburn - Shildon (and one passenger train on Sundays).

By 1870, the passenger service would comprise nine trains in the Down direction (the 11:15 pm Darlington – Middlesbrough only stopping when required), and two on Sundays. Goods for Fighting Cocks from stations to the west would be worked by a Darlington Pilot Engine, departing Darlington at 12:30 pm and timetabled to return at 1 pm. In the Up direction, the station would be served by nine passenger trains and three goods, the 8:20 am Middlesbrough - Tow Law, the 11:15 am Saltburn - Crook and the Loftus Goods (4:10 pm Middlesbrough – Darlington) (and two passenger trains on Sundays). (DJ Williamson Collection)

second station serving Darlington, at Bank Top, on what was now the North Eastern's main line. Due to geographical constraints, and the fact that the line had been built as a main north – south trunk route, this second station was not particularly close to Darlington's town centre either. But it was a lot closer than North Road. In conjunction with the enlargement of Bank Top station in 1887, the North Eastern's directors decided to construct a branch from the main line at Darlington eastwards to a junction with the former S&DR's main line some 4 miles distant. The new branch would expedite passenger traffic in particular between Darlington Bank Top, Stockton and Middlesbrough.

The new branch was opened for traffic on 1 July 1887. As noted above, it formed the western end of the North Eastern's Darlington & Saltburn Branch. The by-passed portion of the former S&DR's main line was designated the Fighting Cocks Branch; it was also described as the Fighting Cocks Loop Line.(3)

A Description of the Fighting Cocks Branch circa 1898

In 1898, the North Eastern published a booklet *Traffic for and from Collieries, Works, Sidings and Depots connected with the North Eastern Railway*. This gives us a useful snapshot of the goods and mineral traffic connected with the Fighting Cocks Branch. There was also, of course, cross-country through goods and mineral traffic. The volume of this is indicated by the fact that Fighting Cocks signal box was open 24 hours per day on weekdays; it was closed all day Sunday, not opening until 6 am on Monday.(4) (Regular passenger traffic need not concern us, as there wasn't any – it had been transferred to Dinsdale station on the Darlington & Saltburn Branch. Stationmaster Eugene Carter Tomkins was transferred from Fighting Cocks to serve as Dinsdale's first stationmaster.)(5)

Starting our survey at the west end of the branch, it commenced at Albert Hill Junction. This junction was where the Parkgate Loop ran west - south to connect with the north - south East Coast Main Line. Much of

Looking eastwards towards S&D Crossing from the site of the original junction of the S&DR's main line to Stockton and the former Croft Depot Branch which veers off to the right. The location was known locally as 'Hill Top House Junction'. S&D Crossing signal box can seen to the left of the line of goods vans in the distance. Looming above the vans is the former Newcastle & Darlington Junction Railway engine shed. (JF Mallon)

the Loop followed the commencement of the S&DR's branch to Croft Depots. In 1898, what had been the beginning of the branch was now multiple tracks. The junction was signalled by Albert Hill Junction signal box.

The first signal box controlling Albert Hill Junction was located on the east side of the bridge spanning the River Skerne. Little is known about it. A drawing dated 1895 labels it 'Old signal cabin'.(6) It may have been a bridge signal box as the drawing shows it with the coal depot line running below (or over the site). No photographs have yet been seen by the authors. The same drawing also shows the box's replacement, located north of the tracks and west of the River Skerne. The replacement had a frame with 77 levers, which would be replaced in 1955 by a frame having only 60 levers. (Albert Hill Junction signal box would close on 21 September 1969.)

The signal box also controlled a west – north curve. This had replaced an earlier curve located a short distance to the west that had served both the South Durham Iron Works as well as linking the S&DR and North Eastern main lines. In 1898, the curve comprised a connecting link and numerous sidings. It appears that the link was used infrequently by 1898, though before the S&DR and North Eastern merger, it had been busy with goods traffic. The Engineer's Line Diagram dated 1903 indicates that by this date the link from the curve to the main line had been severed.

The Fighting Cocks Branch crossed the main line on the level 512 yards from Albert Hill Junction. The intersection of the two railways was named S&D Crossing. Being a place fraught with hazard, it was signalled from the day that traffic first began to use it. The Stockton & Darlington and the Newcastle & Darlington Junction Railways agreed upon a set of regulations – these included provision of a red board signal (which displayed a red light at night) and a speed limit of 10 mph on both lines. As a general rule, N&DJR trains had priority over those of the S&DR, though passenger trains had priority over coal trains.(7) The nature of the initial accommodation provided for the 'bobbies' manning the signals at S&D Crossing is not known. In the mid 1860s, a substantial signal box on a stone base was built and fitted with a Saxby & Farmer 23-lever frame. Contemporary practice was for the signals to be mounted on posts protruding through the roof of the signal box. This box was visited in 1872 by a reporter from *The Northern Echo*, who compiled an account of the box, its equipment and the men who manned it.(8) The signal box was named 'Crossings'(by 1922 changed to 'S&D Crossing').

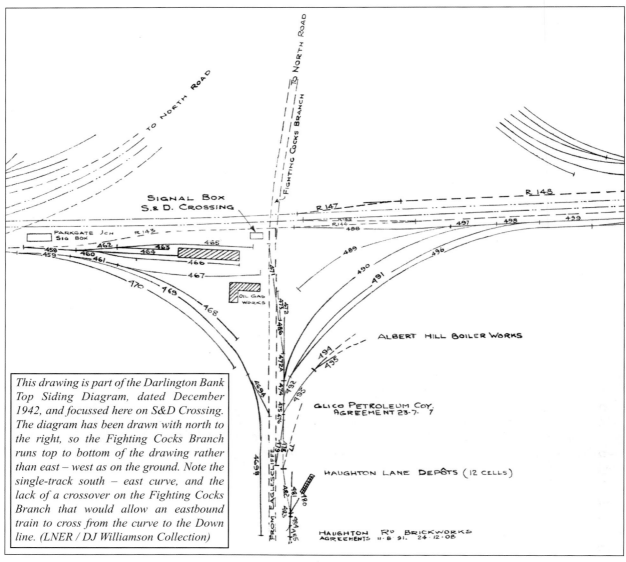

This drawing is part of the Darlington Bank Top Siding Diagram, dated December 1942, and focussed here on S&D Crossing. The diagram has been drawn with north to the right, so the Fighting Cocks Branch runs top to bottom of the drawing rather than east – west as on the ground. Note the single-track south – east curve, and the lack of a crossover on the Fighting Cocks Branch that would allow an eastbound train to cross from the curve to the Down line. (LNER / DJ Williamson Collection)

8

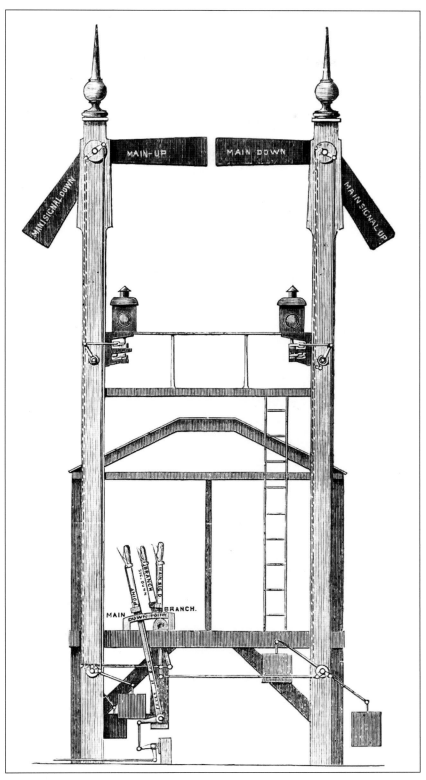

The first shelter provided for the 'bobbies' working the red board signal protecting S&D Crossing was probably nothing more than a rude hut. In the mid 1860s, however, Saxby & Farmer was commissioned by the S&DR to build a proper signal box. Saxby & Farmer's practice at the time to was to mount the signals on posts protruding from the roof of the box; this minimised the rodding required between lever and signal, though it did mean that signals were some distance from the places where trains were required to stop. This drawing of a Saxby & Farmer signal box was published in 'The Engineer' dated 8 March 1861,

though it may be from John Saxby's interlocking signalling patent application. The patent was for a system that mechanically interlocked points and signals. In the past, accidents had been caused by points and signals, operated by independent levers, being set at variance to each other. Saxby devised a system whereby all the point and signal levers under the control of a cabin were interlocked. Neither an individual set of points and its associated signal, nor the entire installation of points and signals, could be set incorrectly.

A MODERN CROSSING MADE OF
HADFIELD'S PATENT 🟊 MANGANESE STEEL
TRADE *ERA* MARK
FOR BRITAIN'S OLDEST ENGLISH RAILWAY
STOCKTON & DARLINGTON SECTION OF THE LONDON & NORTH EASTERN RAILWAY
DESIGNED AND CONSTRUCTED BY
HADFIELDS LTD., SHEFFIELD

Hadfield's make the most of the glamour surrounding the LNER's new streamlined 'Silver Jubilee', seen here hauled by Class A4 No 2510 'Quicksilver'. The train, a London-bound working, is passing over S&D Crossing. The first public run by the train was on 1 October 1935 with seven carriages in the formation as in the photograph; an eighth carriage would soon be added to meet passenger demand. (DJ Williamson Collection)

The following three photographs of S&D Crossing appear to have been taken circa 1924 to record the replacement of the track at the crossing; note the new ballast. Here, the Fighting Cocks Branch runs from upper left to bottom right. The three tracks on the main line comprise the Independent (later designated Up Slow, nearest the camera), the Up Main and the Down Main. The view is looking approximately north-west. (LNER / NERA Collection CE071)

This view looks westwards along the Fighting Cocks Branch back towards Albert Hill Junction. S&D Crossing signal box is to the left. (LNER / NERA Collection CE070)

This view looks eastwards along the Fighting Cocks Branch. S&D Crossing signal box is to the right. Beyond is the end of the former NER Oil Gas Plant which supplied gas for carriage lighting via a $1\frac{1}{2}''$ main to Northgate Carriage Sidings. Beyond that can be seen the rear of the NER platelayers' cottages built in 1884. (LNER / NERA Collection CE067)

Bound for Darlington Bank Top station, Class A8 No 69891 works a diverted Saltburn - Darlington passenger train round the south – east curve at S&D Crossing some time in the 1950s. (Note that the train is running round the curve in the direction east to south.) Parkgate signal box is to the left of the train. S&D Crossing signal box is beyond in the middle distance. (JW Armstrong / Armstrong Railway Photographic Trust)

In 1881, the Saxby frame was replaced by an 18 lever frame. By this time, signals were placed trackside at the locations were trains were required to stop. The upper part of the box may have been replaced in brick at this time, built upon the original stone base. The 1881 frame was replaced in 1898 by a 5 inch pitch Central Division-pattern frame having 31 levers. It may have been at this time that a timber bay window was built on to the north side of the signal box to increase the space within and thus allow the signalman to pass round the end of new frame and thus access the windows for cleaning. (The bay window is not present in the photograph on page 14, taken in 1891.)

The opening hours of Crossings signal box are listed in the *Appendix B* of the 1897 issue to the *General Rules and Regulations…* Seven days a week, the box was always open.

In 1908, the signalling arrangements at S&D Crossing were changed. Prior to this date, the signal box controlled signals on both the S&DR and the NER main lines. After the changes were made, the signal box controlled signals on the former S&DR only. These could only be cleared once the signals on the NER main line had been locked in the 'danger' position by the signalman at Parkgate signal box (located south of S&DR Crossing on the NER main line.) The simplification of the signalling was intended to save £114 a year by allowing S&DR Crossing box to be closed overnight and on Sundays, and by downgrading the status of the box from Passenger to Goods and reducing the signalmen's rate of pay accordingly.

Crossings / S&D Crossing signal box controlled also a north – east curve and a south – east curve. The north – east curve was not yet in place when the area was surveyed by the Ordnance Survey in 1855, though it appears to have been installed not long

afterwards. It was known by generations of railwaymen as the 'Ironstone Curve' as such traffic had used it in the 1860s. However, this traffic had run for a few years only, and appears to have been re-routed on or shortly after 1 July 1865. Such was the institutional memory of railwaymen… By 1898, the curve was used little if at all as a connection between the former S&DR and the main line, but was used for access to industrial premises. By 1903, the curve's connection to the main line had been severed. It must have been re-instated some time, possibly as a wartime expedient, as during the Second World War there was a regular working of limestone (used as a flux in blast furnaces) from Aycliffe Quarry via the Ironstone Curve to Teesside.

The south – east curve was already in place when the Ordnance Survey began its mapping of the area in 1855 – the map was published in 1858. By circa 1898 – and possibly a lot earlier – the curve had a connection only to the Up line of the Fighting Cocks Branch (*i.e.* the line used by westbound traffic). The 1896 revision of the 25 inch Ordnance Survey (published in 1898) shows a crossover connecting Down and Up lines so that a train coming off the curve from the south and heading east could reach the Down line. At the same location was a crossover connecting sidings serving Bridge Works, Haughton Road coal depot and Haughton Road Brick Works to the Down line. Traffic to and from these locations was dealt with by Darlington (Hope Town) goods station. Haughton Road (originally known as Haughton Lane) was the former Darlington to Stockton turnpike, and the coal depot here had been in place since S&DR days along with a level crossing and a gate house. By 1898, however, the road no longer crossed the railway on the level but via an underpass.

No 7 is typical of the long-boiler 0-6-0s the S&DR was using to haul mineral and goods trains circa 1898 (though it was no longer new by then). It was built at North Road Works, Darlington, entering traffic in June 1869 (taking the number of an earlier No 7). The inside cylinders were 17" bore x 24" stroke; wheels were 5' 0½" diameter. No 7 would be withdrawn in 1909.

Early in the morning of 12 February 1875, a locomotive of this type (it is not identified in the records) departed Shildon with a special mineral train bound for Middlesbrough. The train comprised 35 mineral wagons; as was usual at the time, there was no guard and no brake van at the rear of the train. The morning was very foggy. At S&D Crossing, the signalman knew that he ought to divert the train into a siding as the 7:45 am Darlington (North Road) - Saltburn passenger train was inevitably going to catch up with it. However, in the fog, he could not see if the siding was empty; he allowed the mineral train to pass.

At this time, block signalling was being installed on the S&DR main line. However, it had not yet been installed on the section North Road - Fighting Cocks. At S&D Crossing, the signalman was despatching trains on the time interval system. A reasonable time having elapsed, or so he supposed, he allowed the passenger train to follow the mineral train into the fog; he did not warn the driver about the train ahead of him. Nor did the signalman at Haughton Lane. The collision occurred just short of Fighting Cocks; 20 passengers suffered minor injuries.(9) (NERA Ken Hoole Collection KH105_106)

No 240 was one of a class of 10 4-4-0s built at North Road Works in October 1872 to work Darlington Section passenger traffic. The locomotive is seen here at Saltburn, carrying the number 1240 as allocated by the NER (which had a No 240 of its own). The outside cylinders were 17" bore x 30" stroke; driving wheel diameter was 7' 1". The locomotive's Achilles Heel was the 13" diameter solid brass piston valves, which tended to seize. In due course the locomotives would be re-built as inside cylinder 2-4-0s with conventional cast-iron slide valves. (NERA Ken Hoole Collection KH105_138)

Railway Collision at Darlington : Another Brake Failure
The Northern Echo, 27 October 1891

An alarming collision occurred between two trains at the Albert Hill crossing about seven o'clock yesterday morning. A mineral train from Shildon to Stockton was approaching the crossing at a pretty fast speed, when the engine driver observed a meat train from Newcastle making for the crossing at the same time. The signal-board was "off" for the mineral train and against the meat train; but when the engine driver of the latter tried to stop the engine the brakes would not act. Both the enginemen and firemen of each engine finding that a collision could not be avoided, jumped from their engines and within a short time the Newcastle engine struck the other engine with great force. Both locomotives were seriously damaged, and several trucks and wagons were also smashed to pieces whilst others were sent off the metals, blocking the road completely. A number of men from the North-road Shops and Bank Top Shops were directly on the spot of the accident and, under the Superintendence of Mr. W. Younghusband and Mr. J. J. Murray commenced to clear away the debris. The breakdown gangs from Newcastle, Darlington and Middlesbrough were also sent for and the main line to Newcastle was cleared after some time had elapsed. The line to Stockton was blocked during most of the day and the passenger line round by Bank Top had to be used until the road was made passable. The damage is estimated to be very considerable but fortunately nobody was injured.

In the above account, William Younghusband was the manager of North Road Works and John J Murray was in charge of Bank Top locomotive shed. Class 901 No 850 was running south on the main line at the head of a meat train when it failed to stop at S&D Crossing. The front end of the locomotive appears to be undamaged, though the entire locomotive has been forced off the main line and on to the Fighting Cocks Branch. Thus it would appear that, despite what the newspaper article states, it was Class 1001 No 1074, which was travelling eastwards at the head of a mineral train for Stockton, that struck No 850 and not vice versa. As No 1074's tender is next to No 850, and its chimney can be seen above the toolboxes on No 850's tender, No 1074 would seem to have been running tender first. (Ken Hoole Study Centre Collection)

The siding agreement for Bridge Works (an ironworks) has not been located. The first siding agreement for Haughton Road Brick Works was signed by the S&DR and William Alexander Wooler circa 1878. Over the years that followed, new agreements were signed as the brickworks changed hands or was sub-let. The NER and J Dawson Fawcett (Darlington) Limited signed a third party agreement on 7 April 1921, allowing an extension of the brickworks siding to serve a newly-established engineering works.(10)

The crossovers and facing connection to the south – east curve were controlled by Haughton Lane signal box, located 899 yards from Albert Hill Junction, slightly further to the east of the former gate house and also on the south side of the line. However, the cost of the crossovers and signal box was evidently deemed too high, as all were abolished. Closure of the signal box was authorised in March 1898, with 'the sidings at present worked from it to be placed under the control of the Signalman at the Crossings Cabin.' The work was estimated to cost £370, offset by savings of 22s 0d per week in signalmen's wages.(11) The crossovers were presumably removed at the same time as the signal box (they certainly do not appear on the Engineer's Line Diagram drawn up in the 1920s). The abolition of the crossover connecting the Up and Down lines indicates that there was little if any south to east traffic over the curve.

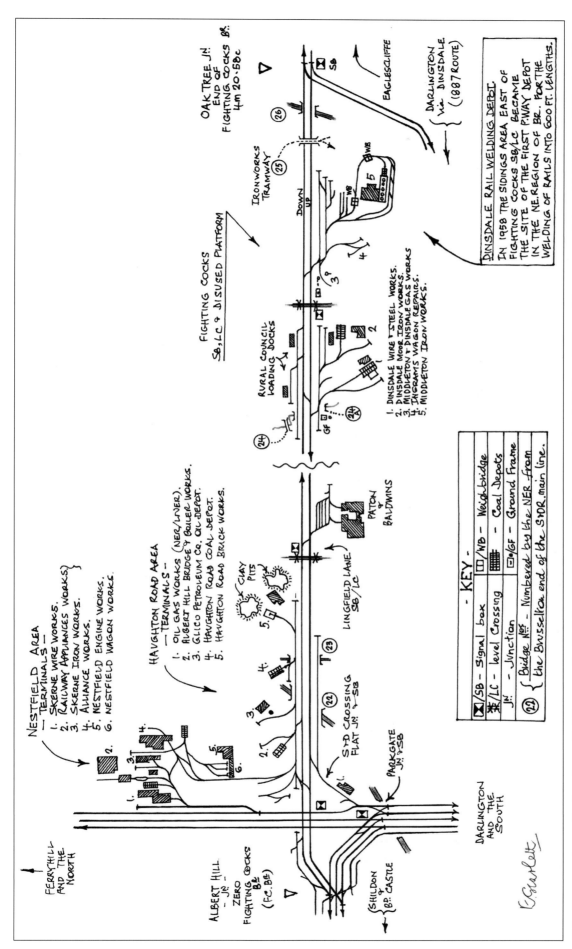

This diagram shows the locations of sidings on the Fighting Cocks Branch; the diagram does not show the branch at a specific period in time. Several of the sidings had multiple users. For example, the sidings labelled '4' at Fighting Cocks seem originally to have served a brickworks owned by HW Graham; the siding agreement was dated 29 June 1899, and it was amended on 17 February 1903 when Messrs Johnson and Boyd took over the works. Charles Frederick Ingram, described as a 'railway wagon builder and repairer', took over the sidings by an agreement signed 9 May 1921. This agreement would run until 5 April 1945. (E Scarlett)

In mid June 1876, Colonel CS Hutchinson, RE, in his capacity as a Board of Trade Inspecting Officer, visited the Fighting Cocks Branch. At the Red Hall block station (located east of Lingfield Lane, and about 1½ miles from S&D Crossing), a new 'passing siding' had been laid and Board of Trade consent was required before it could be used. The siding was on the Up (westbound) side of the line, joining the branch via a trailing connection. Thus a train needing to use it – in order to allow a faster train to pass – had to shunt in backwards. Hutchinson ordered that a buffer stop be provided at the end of the siding, and with that proviso gave his consent. The siding was not in use for long, the signals and switches (the trailing connection to the Up line and a trap point) being removed circa May 1879.(12)

Red Hall signal box (which took its name from the nearby Red Hall) was also on the Up side of the line just west of the trailing connection. It had a frame of 8 to 10 levers, probably supplied by the local firm of Charles I'Anson & Son. Despite the removal of the signals and switches in 1879, the building may have been left in place; it reappears in the 1885 *Appendix* which shows that it was then only open from 6 am to 6 pm during the working week (closed on Sundays). It does not appear in the 1889 *Appendix*; when passenger traffic moved on to the new line through Dinsdale in 1887 it was no longer required.

In 1898, the next signal box beyond that at Haughton Lane (as noted above, in March 1898 condemned to closure) was Fighting Cocks, at 3 miles 769 yards from Albert Hill Junction. This appears to have originally been Fighting Cocks East, the counterpart to Fighting Cocks West (they were 770 yards apart), but by 1887 the latter had closed. Fighting Cocks signal box was to the style designated in modern times 'Type C1b', with panelled brickwork on the ground floor, dating it to the mid 1880s. It may have been erected to replace both East and West boxes, as the lever frame was noted as dating from 1886. The frame had 19 levers, was to a Central Division design, and was probably supplied by I'Anson. A separate wheel was provided to operate the level crossing gates.

The S&DR had built a station here in 1830, and named it Middleton and Dinsdale.(13) The NER had re-built it and re-named it Fighting Cocks circa 1866, and closed it to passengers in 1887; passenger traffic had been re-directed to Dinsdale station on the Darlington & Saltburn Branch. For the last full year of passenger traffic, Fighting Cocks had booked 27,461 passengers which had earned the company £1006.

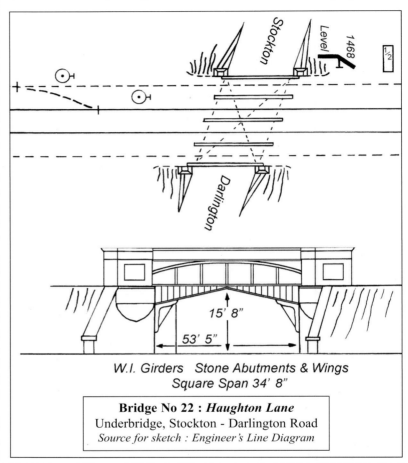

W.I. Girders   Stone Abutments & Wings
Square Span 34' 8"

Bridge No 22 : *Haughton Lane*
Underbridge, Stockton - Darlington Road
Source for sketch : Engineer's Line Diagram

Bridge No 22, Haughton Road, photographed circa 1954 and subsequent to its re-building with new steel girders; date of re-building not known. A Class A8 runs over the bridge with a diverted Sunday Darlington (Bank Top) - Saltburn train. (JW Armstrong / Armstrong Railway Photographic Trust)

16

Haughton Road Coal Depot Agent's house and office, photographed in a ruinous condition in the 1950s. In 1893 the coal depot had been particulary busy, handling 25,838 tons of 'Coal, Coke, Lime and Limestone'. Given the depot's location, it is presumed that little if any of this was agricultural lime, and most if not all was coal. This tonnage was freakishly large, possibly for an industrial concern that subsequently took deliveries direct. Typical annual tonnages were 3827 tons in 1892 and 5160 tons in 1894.(14) (JW Armstrong / Armstrong Railway Photographic Trust)

Lingfield Lane Crossing as photographed in 1948, looking south. Until the arrival of the Patons & Baldwins textile factory (to be described later in the chapter) Lingfield Lane was just a bridleway, exceedingly muddy in winter. It crossed the Fighting Cocks Branch via this unsupervised crossing whose gates were invariably left open. (J Coulthard)

An additional £97 had been earned from 'Parcels, Horses, Carriages, Dogs, &c.' In 1898, however, Fighting Cocks was still a busy goods station. Traffic in 'Coal, Coke, Lime, and Limestone' amounted to 8548 tons. 'Goods Forwarded' totalled 10,495 tons and 'Goods Received' 12,677 tons. Traffic was handled in three sets of sidings.

North of Fighting Cocks there were sidings on both sides of the line. The sidings accessed from the Up (*i.e.* westbound) line, and a main line crossover, were worked by a 2-lever ground frame. The presumption is, that the ground frame replaced Fighting Cocks West signal box; the key to this frame was kept in Fighting Cocks signal box. The sidings gave access to: a brick and tile works; Dinsdale Wire & Steel Works; William Richards' Dinsdale Moor Iron Works; Fighting Cocks goods station's loading dock (with a 1 ton crane), coal cells and warehouse. On the other side of the railway, accessed from the Down line, were further sidings and a loading dock. Fighting Cocks Manure Siding may have been here, though its exact location has not been determined. A siding agreement between the NER and the Rural District Council would be signed on 21 July 1913; the dock would be used to load slag tarmacadam for use in road repair.

South of Fighting Cocks, a third set of sidings was accessed from the Up line, though there was an associated crossover on the main line for use by trains coming from the Darlington direction on the Down line. In 1898, these sidings gave access to: Alderson's Siding; Middleton & Dinsdale Gas Works; Joseph Torbock's Middleton Iron Works. The first of these has not been located, but may have been a siding which ran behind the platform at Fighting Cocks goods station (included in '3' on the diagram on page 15). On 22 May 1903, the NER and RW Rundle signed an agreement pertaining to this siding; RW Rundle & Company were iron and steel merchants and manufacturers. The agreement was revised on 19 November 1909 to allow use of the siding by TW Atkinson who was described as a 'Stone Concrete Manufacturer'.

Fighting Cocks goods station was also responsible for the traffic to coal and lime cells at Low Goosepool, though these were now on the Darlington & Saltburn Branch – they had been relocated when the new branch was constructed, as they had originally been situated very close to the site of Oak Tree Junction.

The branch terminated at Oak Tree Junction, 4 miles 453 yards from Albert Hill Junction. Oak Tree signal box opened in 1 July 1887 as a consequence of the opening of the new line from Darlington. It was built in a similar style to those at Geneva, Coundon and Byers Green, all from the same period. The box had 18 levers (numbered 0 and 1 to 17), and the frame was of the early Central Division pattern with flat floor plates and raised lever guides as also seen at Fighting Cocks.

When this print of Fighting Cocks was published in 1875, the station was at its busiest; the view is looking in the Stockton direction. The chimneys in the left background form part of Middleton Iron Works. By 1875, the Stockton & Darlington Railway had been absorbed into the North Eastern Railway, but was still operated more or less independently as the NER's Darlington Section. Fighting Cocks would lose its passenger traffic in July 1887 upon the opening of the line via Dinsdale, but would retain its goods and mineral traffic. (London Illustrated Weekly News)

According to the Working Time Table in effect 1 October 1897 to 30 April 1898, the sidings on the Fighting Cocks Branch were served from the Darlington end by two timetabled trains. The 7:30 am North Road Goods ran to Middlesbrough; timetabled departure from Fighting Cocks was 8:15 am. The second Goods train ran as required from North Road to Fighting Cocks; departure time from North Road was 12:35 pm, with arrival timetabled for 12:45. Timetabled allowance for shunting was 1 hour 35 minutes; departure time was 2:20 pm, with 10 minutes allowed for the run back to North Road.

Two timetabled trains served the branch from the other direction. The 10:50 am Saltburn Goods to North Road stopped at Fighting Cocks as required. The second train ran at different times during the period of the timetable. The 5:40 pm from Middlesbrough Goods to North Road did not run on 4 October 1897 nor on alternate Mondays. The 5:45 pm Saltburn Goods to North Road ran on 4 October 1897, and on alternate Mondays. Trains stopped at Fighting Cocks as required. There was no goods service on Sundays.

Dinsdale Moor Iron Works

These were established in 1860 by a consortium of businessmen, including members of the Pease family (who had been instrumental in the creation of the S&DR), HAW Cocks (the Lord of the Manor, and whose family is thought to have given rise to the name Fighting Cocks) and JW Wooler (a Darlington colliery owner). Iron was worked at Dinsdale Moor Iron Works,

Fighting Cocks in 1933, with the platforms removed and the railway fenced off from the station buildings; in 1933, these latter are still occupied as housing and offices. (JW Armstrong / Armstrong Railway Photographic Trust)

WD Class No 90014 and a brake van pass Fighting Cocks signal box in June 1964. (RB Coulthard)

Fighting Cocks signal box in June 1964. Signalman Barker is replacing the gate stop lever, with the massive gate wheel behind him. He had been transferred to Fighting Cocks after closure of the Simpasture Branch in 1963 resulted in working two shifts (see page 28). (RB Coulthard)

not made there. The site of the ironworks was some distance from the blast furnaces that produced the required pig iron, but of course the existence of the railway meant that transport could be effected economically. Presumably, the reason that the ironworks was sited at Fighting Cocks specifically was because the Cocks family owned the land and it could thus be provided cheaply to the consortium.

By 1908, the Dinsdale Moor Iron Works was owned by William Richards (later joined in the business by his sons), and the major buildings on the site included a rolling mill.(15) Adjacent to the ironworks was Dinsdale Wire & Steel Works, owned by the Dinsdale Wire & Steel Company.

In 1931 (the siding agreement with the LNER was dated 11 July), WH Arnott, Young & Company Limited took over the site hitherto occupied by the Dinsdale Wire & Steel Company as a scrapyard – one of several the company established across the UK. A fan of four widely-spaced sidings, complete with weighbridge and weigh office, was laid. On 15 April 1948, a supplementary agreement was signed; henceforth BR locomotives would shunt the sidings, charging 25 shillings per hour so to do. Many BR steam locomotives were scrapped there in the 1960s. In 1980 Arnott, Young was taken over by TJ Thompson & Son Limited. The sidings at Fighting Cocks were re-assigned to Dinsdale Metal Processors Limited. (The siding agreement would be terminated with effect from 7 February 1983.)

Middleton Iron Works

Middleton Iron Works was established in 1864 by the Middleton Iron Works Company in what from 1887 would be the vee of land where the Fighting Cocks and the Darlington & Saltburn Branches joined. It was named for the nearby township of Middleton St George. It was a long way from sources of raw materials: ironstone, coal and limestone flux. Presumably the reason that the site was chosen was that a large acreage of cheap land was available, both for the ironworks itself and the huge heaps of blast furnace slag that would be produced in the future. As was the case with Dinsdale Moor Iron Works, the railway would provide economical transport of raw materials in and of pig iron out. Two blast furnaces were erected, served by an internal railway system. One furnace was put into blast in 1865, and both were in blast for at least part of 1866. However, it would appear that profits were insufficient to compensate for the sum invested in setting up the ironworks. The Middleton Iron Works Company got into financial difficulties, and the fires in the blast furnaces went out in 1866.

The ironworks remained idle until they were bought by George Wythes & Company in 1870. The company was a partnership made up of George Wythes himself, John Cochrane, Henry Cochrane and Harry Herbert Cochrane. The partners erected a third blast furnace, and all were put to work. In 1874, a fourth blast furnace was erected, though it was not until 1875 that all four were in blast. An economic downturn led to the shutdown of all four towards the end of 1876.

FIGHTING COCKS.

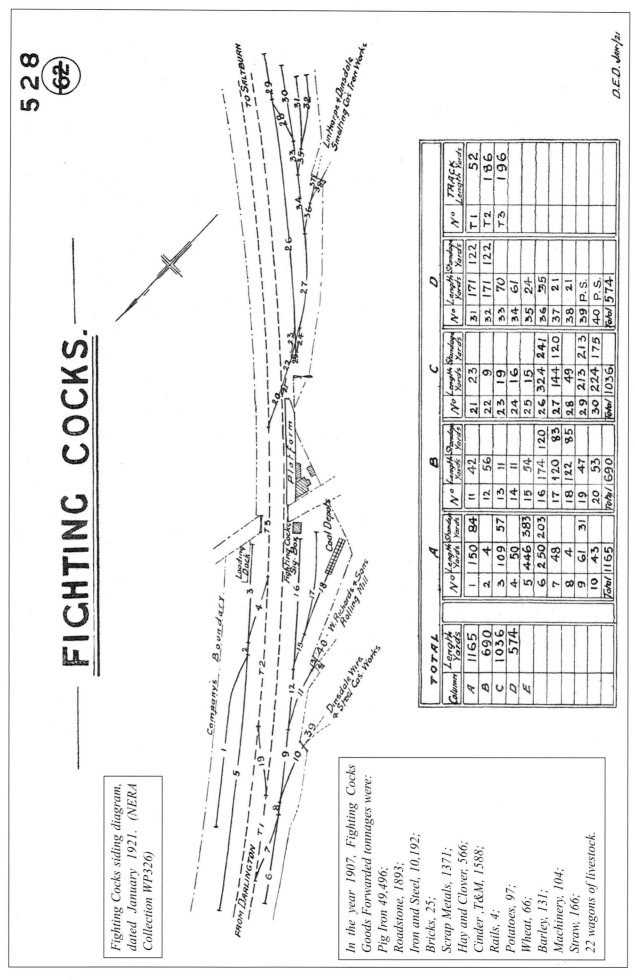

Fighting Cocks siding diagram, dated January 1921. (NERA Collection WP326)

In the year 1907, Fighting Cocks Goods Forwarded tonnages were:

Pig Iron 49,496;
Roadstone, 1893;
Iron and Steel, 10,192;
Bricks, 25;
Scrap Metals, 1371;
Hay and Clover, 566;
Cinder ,T&M, 1588;
Rails, 4;
Potatoes, 97;
Wheat, 66;
Barley, 131;
Machinery, 104;
Straw, 166;
22 wagons of livestock.

D.E.O. Jan/21

TOTAL			A			B			C			D			TRACK	
Column	Length Yards		Nº	Length Yards	Standage Yards	Nª	Length Yards	Standage Yards	Nº	Length Yards	Standage Yards	Nº	Length Yards	Standage Yards	Nº	Length Yards
A	1165		1	150	84	11		42	21		23	31	171	122	T1	52
B	690		2	4		12		56	22		9	32	171	122	T2	186
C	1036		3	109	57	13		11	23		19	33	70		T3	196
D	574		4	50		14		11	24		16	34	61			
E			5	446	383	15		54	25		15	35	24			
			6	250	203	16	174	120	26	324	241	36	35			
			7	48		17	120	83	27	144	120	37	21			
			8	4		18	122	85	28	49		38	21			
			9	61	31	19	47		29	213	213	39	P.S.			
			10	43		20	53		30	224	175	40	P.S.			
			Total 1165			Total 690			Total 1036			Total 574				

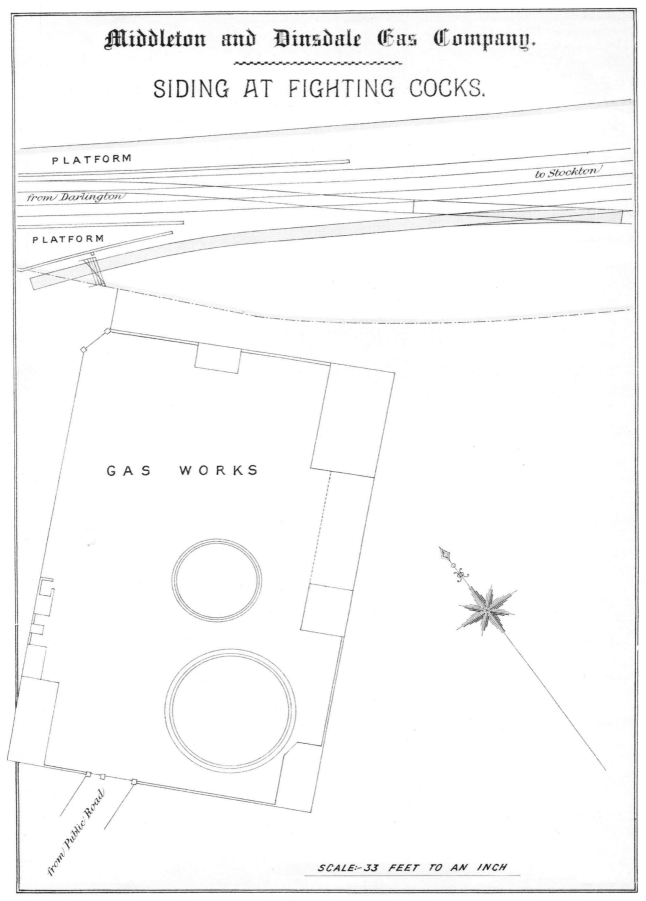

Middleton and Dinsdale Gas Company.

SIDING AT FIGHTING COCKS.

PLATFORM

to Stockton

from Darlington

PLATFORM

GAS WORKS

from Public Road

SCALE:- 33 FEET TO AN INCH

This plan forms part of the siding agreement dated 23 April 1892. One of those entrepreneurs who formed the gas company was Thomas Ness, a manufacturing chemist. Another of his companies, Thomas Ness Limited, owned the Black Banks Chemical Works on the Croft Depot Branch. The local availability of gas at Fighting Cocks allowed the NER to use it to light the signals, including the ground signals. (DJ Williamson Collection)

Class E5 (NER 1463 Class) No 1466 is seen here in the mid 1920s working an inspection saloon over the Fighting Cocks Branch. (The locomotive would be withdrawn in January 1927.) The train is on the Up line north of Fighting Cocks station where the line curves round South Burdon Farm. (NERA Collection)

Possibly also as a consequence of the downturn, the partnership was dissolved on 1 December 1877. George Wythes retained ownership of the Middleton Iron Works, and two of the blast furnaces were put back into blast in 1881. George Wythes died in 1882, and his executors continued to manage the ironworks. 1883 was a good year, with all four furnaces in blast. However, all four blast furnaces shut down the following year.

In 1891, Middleton Iron Works was purchased by Joseph Torbock. The blast furnaces remained cold and idle. In 1900 Torbock sold the ironworks to the Dinsdale Smelting Company Limited. It was not until the following year that one of the furnaces was re-commissioned and put back into blast. On 3 April 1903, the company merged with the Linthorpe Iron Works to form the Linthorpe & Dinsdale Smelting Company Limited. Linthorpe Iron Works had six blast furnaces, so the combined company had ten. 1907 was a particularly productive year for the Middleton furnaces, 49,496 tons of pig iron being produced. Production fluctuated according to demand, falling to 31,687 tons the following year.

Until the outbreak of war in 1914, one, two or three of the Middleton furnaces were in blast, though never all four. It is likely that all four were in blast during the war years, though it is not possible to be certain as detailed statistics were not published.

In 25 May 1920, a new company was registered: the Linthorpe-Dinsdale Smelting Company Limited. Production figures for the Middleton furnaces in 1925 and 1927 were 27,569 tons and 24,054 tons.(16)

The ironworks at Linthorpe shut down in May 1930, leaving only the Middleton furnaces in blast. These shut down for good in August 1946 when the Linthorpe-Dinsdale Smelting Company Limited went into voluntary liquidation. Circa March 1947, WH Arnott, Young & Company Limited began to dismantle the ironworks; the blast furnaces were demolished in April 1948.

The Middleton Iron Works had, over the years, generated a huge amount of blast furnace slag. This had been tipped in the vee between the two railway branches. Overbridges had also been built over both branches, and the ironworks' internal railway extended over them in order to access slag tipping grounds in the open fields beyond. On 6 July 1927, Clokes Extension Limited, which was processing the slag heaps in order to produce material for road-building, signed an agreement with the LNER allowing it to erect another bridge over the Fighting Cocks Branch. This bridge was to carry a 2 feet gauge narrow gauge railway, to be used to bring slag from the heaps to the processing plant.(17) The signalling diagram for Fighting Cocks signal box dated 5 February 1965 includes the label 'Slag Plant Sidings', so they may still have been in use for that purpose at that date. Land in the vee cleared of slag was subsequently used by British Railways as the site of Dinsdale Rail Welding Depot; this will be described below.

Later Developments

Reflecting the increase in the use of petroleum spirit by motor vehicles in particular, in 1927 Glico Petroleum Limited built a depot on Barton Street, Darlington (just off Haughton Road, a few yards north of where the road passed beneath the Fighting Cocks Branch. The LNER laid in a short siding to serve the depot – siding and depot were connected via a pipeline. The siding agreement was dated 23 July 1927.(18)

During the period of the timetable current 8 April - 7 July 1929, the sidings on the Fighting Cocks Branch were served from the Darlington end by four trains.

The 6:22 am North Road Class D Goods was timetabled to arrive at Albert Hill at 6:27 am. Half an hour was allowed for shunting the various sidings in the vicinity, then it was on to Fighting Cocks; arrival time was 7:12 am. From Fighting Cocks, at 7:27 am the train ran on to Newport Sidings serving various sidings en route. The 1:15 pm North Road Class B Goods ran direct to Fighting Cocks. The 4:5 pm (Saturdays Only) Albert Hill Class B Goods shunted at Albert Hill until 4:50 pm, then proceeded to Fighting Cocks. Half an hour was allowed for shunting, and at 5:15 pm the train departed for Newport Sidings, calling at other locations en route. The 5:45 pm (Mondays and Saturdays Excepted) Class B Goods shunted at Albert Hill, Fighting Cocks (half an hour) and locations beyond, terminating at Newport Sidings. Fighting Cocks was also served by the 8:10 am Shildon - Fighting Cocks Mineral train; this train did not run directly to Fighting Cocks, but served other locations on the way. After an hour and a half allowed for shunting the various sidings at Fighting Cocks, the return working with empty mineral wagons departed at 10:20 am.

In the opposite direction, Fighting Cocks was served by the 7:5 am Stockton - North Road Class C Goods; the 10:30 am Newport Sidings - North Road Class D Goods; the 1:50 pm (Saturdays Only) Middlesbrough Goods Yard - North Road Class A Goods; the 3:47 pm Fighting Cocks - North Road Class B Goods; the 8:39 pm Stockton - North Road Class C Goods.

The LNER's 1947 *General Appendix to the Rules and Regulations…* informed train crews that advantage had been taken of the fact that only goods and mineral trains regularly used the Fighting Cocks Branch; Albert Hill Junction to Oak Tree Junction was now worked on the Permissive Block System. (It is not known when this change was put into effect, though it may have been a wartime measure introduced circa 1939.) Most of the LNER was worked on the Absolute Block System, which mandated that only one train was allowed in any signalling block section at any one time.(19) In contrast, more than one train was allowed when working the Permissive Block System. Engine drivers were required to drive their trains at a speed at which it was possible to stop safely if a train was seen on the line ahead.

Patons & Baldwins Limited

In 1945, building work began of a state-of-the-art factory for Patons & Baldwins on a 140 acre greenfield site to the south of the line adjacent to Lingfield Lane. The LNER and the company signed a siding agreement on 20 February 1947, and the factory opened in December 1947, though it took a while longer before it was in full production. Raw material (wool) was conveyed inwards by rail, and the finished product (yarn) conveyed outwards. Wagons laden with raw materials and coal for the factory's boilers were worked inwards by the enginemen working Darlington shed's roster D3 each weekday morning, departing Albert Hill at 10:15. Vans loaded with yarn were worked out of the factory by the Nestfield Pilot (roster D13) at 5 pm each weekday; the vans were routed via the east - south curve at S&D Crossing to Bank Top. Building work on the factory was completed in 1951. At its peak production, the factory despatched 113 tons of yarn every week. Sometimes, such was the volume of

Lingfield Lane Crossing, looking east, in 1950. By 1950 road traffic accessing Patons & Baldwins factory (seen in the right background) was sufficiently heavy to justify employing a crossing keeper complete with hut who survived until the construction of a signal box in April 1955. Red Hall Farms, now lost beneath a housing estate, are in view on the left. (JW Armstrong / Armstrong Railway Photographic Trust)

production, two trains were required in an afternoon to take away the loaded vans.

As well as increasing traffic on the railway, the Patons & Baldwins factory increased traffic on the local roads. The factory was adjacent to Lingfield Lane, a muddy bridleway at the time. Since the closure of Red Hall signal box, there had been no signalman or crossing keeper, and the gates were customarily left open. (They closed across the bridleway only, not across the railway, so could be left open without inconvenience to anybody.) By 1950, the number of pedestrians using Lingfield Lane had increased to such an extent that British Railways erected a timber hut and installed a crossing keeper to work the gates. In 1951, the Durham County Agricultural Show was

scheduled to be held on 3 and 4 August in fields adjacent to Lingfield Lane. In anticipation of extra road traffic, the lane was straightened and a temporary level crossing installed a few yards west of the existing crossing; this was protected by a set of field type wooden gates. When the show was over, the crossing went out of use until it was upgraded to a permanent crossing, with standard white-painted crossing gates and wicket gates for pedestrians. Signals were installed on the Up and Down lines to protect the permanent level crossing, which was commissioned in October 1953. The signals were worked by the crossing keeper from a ground frame; the crossing gates were worked by hand.

Some time in 1952, Class J27 No 65860 with the morning pick-up goods working pauses at Lingfield Lane Crossing to hand to the crossing keeper (Mr Stairmand) his supply of fresh water and to throw off some coal for his fire. The locomotive has visited the sidings at Fighting Cocks and Messrs Patons & Baldwins and will run on to Albert Hill and subsequently work the Croft Depot Branch with a new crew. (JW Armstrong / Armstrong Railway Photographic Trust)

Lingfield Lane Crossing Keeper Stairmand only had telephone contact with the signalman at Fighting Cocks, who advised him of traffic movements etc. Stairmand never spoke to the signalmen at the west end of the line. On one memorable occasion the Fighting Cocks signalman was taken ill and rushed to hospital; the branch closed prematurely with traffic going via Dinsdale. Nobody advised Stairmand at Lingfield Lane. He loyally stuck to his post, afraid that if he departed and a train subsequently came there could be serious consequences. Very late at night (he usually finished by 5 pm on Saturdays then) he waved down a passing cycling policeman who alerted the railway authorities at Bank Top.

By the time this photograph was taken, some time after October 1953, the original crossing at Lingfield Lane is out of use and the gate closed. Partly visible to the left is the road that replaced it. The ground frame used by the crossing keeper to work the signals protecting the new road crossing is just to the right of the trespass warning sign, on the other side of the wire fence. (JW Armstrong / Armstrong Railway Photographic Trust

The sidings at Patons & Baldwins were accessed via the Up line; the ground frame containing the point lever was locked when not in use, the key being kept at S&D Crossing signal box. There was no crossover here, so trains bound for the factory from Albert Hill, approaching on the Down line, had to continue on past to the crossover at Fighting Cocks. Having changed tracks at Fighting Cocks, the trains returned via the Up line.

In 1955, a new signal box was built at Lingfield Lane level crossing, north of the lines and east of the road. This had been planned for some time with drawings produced in 1950.(20) The box opened on 21 April 1955 and was to the current BR (North Eastern Region) design, built of brick with a flat roof and large steel-framed windows. (This design was designated 'Type 16b' by students of signalling history.) The No 16 pattern frame had 21 levers and a wheel to operate the level crossing gates. The signal box never carried a nameboard, and was never fitted with block instruments, only bells. The Patons & Baldwins ground frame was released from the signal box, which became a new block post, though the branch continued to be worked by Permissive Block. A crossover worked from the signal box was also installed, allowing trains on the Down line to cross to the Up, and thus access Patons & Baldwins directly without having to go to Fighting Cocks.

Dinsdale Rail Welding Depot

Prior to the Second World War, the standard length for rails in the UK was 60 feet. In 1939, one of the Southern Railway's civil engineers published a paper on the experiments conducted both on the SR and in the USA on the behaviour of long-welded rails.(21)

These comprised lengths of rail formed by butt-welding end to end 60 feet rails. When laid on the railway, long-welded rail was stronger than 60 feet rails, wore better and was less prone to breakage as there were fewer rail joints, and gave a better ride. After the war, the experiments continued, particularly on BR's London Midland Region and on the underground lines of the London Transport Executive. In 1957, British Railways felt that enough experience had been gained to issue a draft code of practice for all of its Regions, and to instruct the Regions each to build a depot where long-welded rail would be produced. The North Eastern Region opened Dinsdale Rail Welding Depot in 1958. It was built in the vee between the Fighting Cocks and the Darlington & Saltburn Branches on land previously used by Middleton Iron Works to dump blast furnace slag. Initially, 60 feet rails were butt-welded end to end into a single rail 300 feet long.

In the mid 1960s, hydraulic rail tensors were developed that were used to stretch long-welded rail to mimic the effect of expansion by heating in hot weather. The stretched rails were butt-welded to the adjacent length of long-welded rail to produce continuously-welded rail (CWR). Dinsdale then began to produce 600 feet as well as 300 feet long-welded rail. The working area where rails were stored and loaded on to wagons was served by a 10 ton overhead crane which could traverse from side to side over a 76 feet 10 inch span. The crane was mounted on a 607 feet long gantry. The depot also produced pre-fabricated track panels, some of which were made using recycled materials. By the 1980s, the depot was producing some 170 miles of track per annum.

Lingfield Lane Crossing and its new signal box, photographed in 1960, looking east. Road traffic here had continued to grow apace and eventually under strong pressure from the Borough Council BR had upgraded the crossing and built this signal box which opened in April 1955. BR also created a Block Post here, though for a long time the branch had been worked under 'Permissive' regulations, and would continue to be so worked. Throughout its relatively short life (it would close in May 1967) the box would never sport external name boards. Although equipped with block bells the signal box would never be endowed with block instruments either. (RB Coulthard)

Steel rail is flexible, so even the 600 feet lengths of long-welded rail could be transported on a special rake of wagons. Eventually, the depot had an allocation of seven such rakes. The depot also had allocated its own departmental shunter to move rakes within the depot; No 82 was a brand new four-wheeled Ruston Hornsby diesel-mechanical. In January 1964, an additional shunter was provided; No 89 was a Hunslet Engine Company diesel-mechanical 0-6-0, first into traffic in 1961 as No D2615. These departmental shunters were re-allocated elsewhere in January 1968 and November 1967 respectively. Thereafter, Thornaby shed provided a shunter on a week by week basis, shunters returning to Thornaby each weekend.(22)

Initially, loaded long-welded rail trains were worked out of the depot via Oak Tree Junction. From January 1961, the trains usually worked out in the opposite direction, traversing the length of the Fighting Cocks Branch, round the tight east - south curve at S&D Crossing to Darlington's East Yard. The trains were signalled 2-6-1 (Out of Gauge Load), and became a feature of Thursday and Friday afternoon workings, prior to departing East Yard over the weekend when re-laying operations took place. Traction was usually provided by Darlington's WD Class 2-8-0s.

Decline in Traffic

Although the opening of the Patons & Baldwins factory gave a great boost to the profitability of rail transport in Darlington, post-war the railways' overall fortunes began a steady decline. More and more goods began to be carried by road transport. Passengers bought their own cars, and travelled less frequently by rail. Consumers of coal, both industrial and domestic, began to use instead electricity, oil or gas. As well as diminishing overall, the nature of the railways' coal traffic began to change too. Old collieries were worked out and closed. New pits were sunk, but they were in different parts of the country to the old ones. New customers were found for coal, but the most important of these were the very large base-load power stations being built post-war. The combination of new collieries and new power stations meant that the traditional routes by which coal was transported were replaced by entirely new ones. As well as old collieries, old factories and ironworks began to close too. Some of these were replaced by new, but many closed for good. All of these changes impacted to a greater or lesser extent upon the Fighting Cocks Branch; traffic levels began to fall.

Such was the reduction in traffic on the Fighting Cocks Branch in particular, that the Down line was often requisitioned for the storage of crippled wagons awaiting attention in the wagon repair shops at Faverdale. Prior to the opening of the signal box at

Class J27 No 65859 works an Up Freight (Tees Yard - Shildon) past Patons & Baldwins in March 1964; the locomotive is struggling at this point, and would subsequently expire at Hopetown. The crossover worked from Lingfield Lane signal box, allowing trains on the Down line to cross to the Up, and thus to access Patons & Baldwins directly without having to go to Fighting Cocks, is clearly seen here. Through freight traffic on the Fighting Cocks Branch had reached a very low level by the early 1960s. Closure of the neighbouring Simpasture Branch in June 1963 saw the residual traffic from this branch re-routed over the Fighting Cocks line with a resulting, albeit brief, boost to traffic with the branch reverting to regular two shift working for the first time in many years. (RB Coulthard)

Lingfield Lane, stored wagons could stretch from Haughton Road bridge nearly as far as Fighting Cocks. After the opening of the signal box and the associated crossover, wagons were henceforth stored only from Lingfield Lane eastwards. When the Fighting Cocks Branch was required for use as a Sunday diversionary route for passenger trains – when the western end of the Darlington & Saltburn Branch was closed for engineering work – Single Line Working with a pilotman was instituted. The *Northern Dales Rail Tour*, run on 4 September 1955, was another example of a passenger train obliged to run wrong line from Albert Hill to Fighting Cocks due to stored wagons.(23)

By the early 1950s, traffic had reduced to such an extent that a suggestion that the double track over S&D Crossing be reduced to single in order to reduce maintenance costs was accepted. A proposal was worked up on paper in 1952, though the singling was done some four years later over the Bank Holiday weekend 26 to 28 May 1956. It was the Up Goods line over the crossing that was lifted.(24)

The *Working Timetable of Freight Trains* in effect 18 June to 9 September 1962 includes neither through freight trains over the Fighting Cocks Branch nor any trains serving sidings along the route, though as noted above, traffic to Patons & Baldwins was timetabled locally. Through mineral trains still ran over the branch, though at much reduced level.

From mid summer 1960 to late winter 1961 there were regular Sunday engineering possessions of the Leeds Northern line south of Eaglescliffe as the viaduct spanning the River Tees at Yarm required substantial repairs. The few passenger trains affected were diverted via the Darlington & Saltburn Branch and the Geneva Curve (the south - east curve connecting the branch and the East Coast Main Line). The northbound passenger trains could not access the curve directly, having to stop on the Down line, reverse over a crossover on to the Up line from where they could run forwards over the curve. Control was wary about the idea of northbound freight trains reversing over the crossover, so they ran further north on the East Coast Main Line to the south - east curve at S&D Crossing and then ran via the Fighting Cocks Branch. Once on the branch, the trains could not access the Down line due to the lack of a facing crossover at Haughton Lane, so worked wrong line, accompanied by a pilotman, to Fighting Cocks. The trains were able to use the crossover at Fighting Cocks to reach the Down line. The diverted trains were hauled by Class B16 4-6-0s and Class V2 2-6-2s. There were no diverted freight trains in the opposite direction.

The usual traction over the branch at this time was provided by Class J26 and J27 0-6-0s, Ivatt 4MT 2-6-0s, WD Class 2-8-0s, Class Q6 0-8-0s and the odd Stockton Class B1 4-6-0. Afternoon workings into Patons & Baldwins were usually in the hands of either a Class J72 or J94 0-6-0T. The first record of a diesel locomotive on the branch (as opposed to a diesel multiple-unit, which were by now commonly seen on Sunday diversions) was on 10 October 1962 when new diesel-electric shunter No D3227 worked the afternoon trip to Patons & Baldwins. However, local workings tended to be steam-hauled until Darlington shed closed to steam on 27 March 1966.

In June 1963, the Simpasture Branch closed – it had been part of the former Clarence Railway route connecting Shildon and Teesside, constructed to compete with the Stockton & Darlington Railway.

Patons & Baldwins Factory Sidings, photographed in 1950. Raw wool from the docks, and coal for the factory power station, arrived by rail. The finished yarn was also despatched by rail. To cope with the volume of rail traffic, the factory had some three and a half miles of internal sidings. The Fighting Cocks Branch can be seen on the left of the photograph; the route of the railway is today occupied by the B6279 road. (RB Coulthard)

In order to work its internal railway Patons & Baldwins bought this fireless locomotive, built in September 1948 by WG Bagnall Limited (Works No 2898). The locomotive was supplied with superheated water (from which steam was generated) by the factory boilers, and this hastily-taken snapshot appears to show the charging point.

This is the new amenities block at Dinsdale Rail Welding Depot, photographed on 8 July 1959. (BR / DJ Williamson Collection)

This view is of the interior of the welding shop at Dinsdale Rail Welding Depot. The machine in the centre of the photograph is a straightening press, used to correct any deformation of rails caused by the welding process. For another view of the depot, see inside the rear cover. (T Horner / NERA Collection TH008)

Left : A length of rail is seen here set up for welding. (T Horner / NERA Collection TH005)

Right : A second rail having been butted up against the first, the weld is made. (T Horner / NERA Collection TH006)

From 24 June, freight and mineral traffic that had been routed via the branch was instead routed via the Fighting Cocks Branch. The extra traffic meant a revision to the hours of the staff concerned. For some time, they had been working a single day shift, 9:30 am to 5:30 pm, with a 12:30 pm finish on Saturdays. However, two shifts per day were now required so that the signal boxes would be manned from 8 am to 10 pm.

The extra traffic itself soon began to diminish. At some time, it is not known exactly when, S&D Crossing signal box was downgraded as so little traffic was using the Fighting Cocks Branch. (This downgrading may even have occurred before the temporary boost to traffic caused by the closure of the Simpasture Branch.) In effect, S&D Crossing box became a ground frame, with its levers released remotely from Parkgate signal box – the next box south of S&D Crossing on the main line. A Parkgate signalman walked along the line to S&D Crossing box when a train arrived that needed to use the crossing.

Closure

Fighting Cocks goods station closed on 9 March 1964.(25) The branch itself was heading towards closure too. Such as the siding agreements pertaining to Haughton Road Brick Works were terminated by British Railways with effect from 14 January 1966 (though traffic may already have ceased before that date). The branch itself closed as a through route on 21 May 1967. Although the Fighting Cocks Branch had been used recently as a Sundays diversionary route for Darlington & Saltburn Branch passenger trains (the section from Oak Tree Junction to Darlington South being closed for engineering works), most of its length was closed to normal freight traffic on that date. One track was lifted, but the other remained in place so that traffic could be worked to and from both Patons & Baldwins and Dinsdale Rail Welding Depot. Both the

factory and the depot were worked from the Oak Tree Junction end of the branch; westwards from Lingfield Lane, the branch was closed.(26) The section of line eastwards from Lingfield Lane to Oak Tree Junction was worked in accordance with the One Train Working regulations. S&D Crossing signal box was closed, and the track at the crossing lifted, on 2 July 1967.(27) S&D Crossing, Lingfield Lane and Fighting Cocks signal boxes were demolished during the week commencing 20 November 1967.(28)

Over the weekend of 7 and 8 October 1972, Oak Tree signal box was abolished and its remaining mechanical semaphore signals replaced by colour lights controlled from Darlington. The Departure Line from Dinsdale Rail Welding Depot to Oak Tree Junction was fully track-circuited, and would henceforth be worked in both directions. (The Arrivals Line was lifted.) An Annetts Key was provided to lock / unlock the points connecting the Departure Line to the Darlington & Saltburn Branch. This same key served also as a train staff for the single track from the depot to Lingfield Lane; it was engraved 'Dinsdale - Lingfield'. When not in Use, the Annetts Key was kept in the Depot supervisor's office.(29)

However, rail traffic from Patons & Baldwins ceased in the early 1970s (the siding agreement was terminated with effect from 5 May 1972). The track from Lingfield Lane to the former Fighting Cocks goods station was closed and lifted. Dinsdale Rail Welding Depot closed in 1988. With the latter closure, the Fighting Cocks Branch closed completely. Part of the route was subsequently built on to form the B6279 road, and the easternmost part is now a public footpath. Sadly, even the historic *Fighting Cocks Inn*, which gave its name to the branch and station, has now been re-branded as *Platform 1*.

Class A8 No 69875 works a Darlington - Saltburn train over Oak Tree Junction some time in 1956; the train is running via Dinsdale and that section of the Darlington & Saltburn Branch opened in 1887. Note that as late as 1956, the junction is protected by an NER lower-quadrant signal. The diesel-electric shunter to the right of the photograph is on the Fighting Cocks Branch. (JW Armstrong / Armstrong Railway Photographic Trust)

The Croft Depot Branch

The Stockton & Darlington Railway Company's Act of 23 May 1823 sanctioned, amongst other things, a branch from Hill House to Croft Bridge; estimated cost was £74,300. The bridge referred to spanned the Tees, and gave road access from County Durham to Richmond and Northallerton and the surrounding agricultural districts in the North Riding of Yorkshire. An S&DR branch to Croft Bridge would expedite the conveyance of coal to those places; in 1818 the promoters of the S&DR had estimated that 10,000 tons of coal per annum would be conveyed over such a branch. Construction was delayed by the Company's financial difficulties – the cost of constructing the S&DR main line had greatly exceeded the original estimates – but once the Black Boy Branch was opened and earning revenue, work could begin. The single-track $3\frac{1}{2}$ miles long Croft Depot Branch was opened for traffic on 27 October 1829. Several proposals from various promoters that the branch be extended over the Tees to Richmond or to York never came to fruition.

The depot that gave its name to the branch was built a short distance from the north end of Croft Bridge in the village of Hurworth Place. It proved to be a useful source of traffic for the S&DR, but within a relatively short time machinations by rival railway promoters had a dramatic effect. The Great North of England Railway (GNER) was promoted as a railway running northwards from York. Running via Northallerton, it would inevitably win to itself a good proportion of the traffic currently conveyed via the Croft Depot Branch. The S&DR Board was therefore quite willing to sell the branch to the GNER, which latter proposed to use much of the northern portion of the branch as a route for its main line. Accordingly, the entire branch changed hands for £20,000 in 1836.

The official opening of the Croft Depot Branch took place on 27 October 1829 when Francis Mewburn, the Stockton & Darlington Railway Company's solicitor, presided over a cold collation at the Croft Spa Hotel. In his obligatory speech Mewburn is reported as having generated considerable mirth when he prophesied 'a day...not far off when a man might lunch in Darlington yet in the same day take in an evening's opera in London'. (NERA Collection)

This is the notorious 'tunnel' on Parkside, Darlington; it appears to be the original S&DR underbridge that carried the Croft Depot Branch. The bridge was subsequently extended to accommodate a double track when this part of the branch became part of the Great North of England Railway, and later extended further using wrought-iron girders to accept more tracks. The bridge is thought to be to the design of Thomas Storey, Assistant Engineer to George Stephenson who was the Engineer responsible for the construction of the S&DR (including the Croft Depot Branch).

The road was subsequently metalled, but its dimensions remain unchanged today creating an irritating east - west town bottleneck. (Centre for Local Studies at Darlington Library)

A vignette from an 1823 S&DR Share Certificate, depicting a horse leading three chaldrons across Bank Top, Darlington, en route to the Croft Depot Branch.

LANDSALE.

WOODHOUSES COLLIERY.

S. & D. R. Co'.s WAY BILL.

20,th day of Nover 1857

Prog. No.	Wagon No.	Weight.	Description.	Destination and who for.
1				
2	6083			
3	4377			
4	5773			
5	4948			
6	11703			
7	3067			
8	8609			
9	4643			
10	2837		Small	St. Helen's Colliery
11	13248		21	
12	13768			
13	6991			
14	540			
15	8331			
16	1077			
17	12140			
18				
19	9217		Bottom	Bishoply Lime Kils
20	6109		Coal. Moff	
21		26		
22	3594		Small	Moff Ord & Madder
23			Coke	
24	8130			
25	8180			
26	5240		Nuts	Croft Depot
27	457			

Left : Part of an S&DR waybill for landsale traffic from Woodhouses Colliery, Bishop Auckland, dated 20 November 1857. At the bottom are listed four wagons of 'Nuts' to be conveyed to Croft Depot. Nuts were pieces of coal sized $1^5/_8$" x $^{13}/_{16}$". (NERA Collection)

From *The Durham Chronicle*, 19 June 1830
Tonnage of coal handled at Croft Depot during the 8 months from opening
Old Black Boy Colliery, 4 cells, 1133 tons.
Shildon Colliery, 4 cells, 1675 tons.
Eldon Colliery, 3 cells, 271 tons.
Old Etherley Colliery, 3 cells, 3357 tons.
New Etherley Colliery, 3 cells, 295 tons.
Witton Park Colliery, 3 cells, 2246 tons.
Deanery Colliery, 1 cell, tonnage not recorded.
Coundon Colliery, 1 cell, 294 tons.
The collieries variously supplied fire coal, small coal and lime coal.

From the notebooks of John Graham, S&DR Traffic Superintendent, 1831 to 1849.
The date of this note is not given, but the incident occurred late June or early July 1832 : 'Between Saturday night and Monday morning some eavel [sic] deposed person or persons had got to William 4th Engine and unscrewed the Spring Valve and took it away from Croft Branch Line.'

1902 was a typical year for traffic to and from Croft Depot. Goods Forwarded totalled 1733 tons, and principally comprised gravel, sand, bricks, timber, hay and clover, barley, potatoes and livestock. Goods Received totalled 2486 tons. In addition, 3890 tons of 'Coal, Coke, Lime and Limestone' were received. Goods Forwarded increased to 6940 tons in 1903 and to 6267 tons in 1904, perhaps due to large shipments of gravel or bricks. Tonnages fell in subsequent years close to that handled in 1902.

In May 1960, Class J27 No 65860 propels four loaded coal wagons over the branch, bound for the coal cells at Croft Depot. Due to the lack of any run-round sidings at the depot, wagons had always to be propelled to the depot, and hauled back to Darlington. (NT Coulthard)

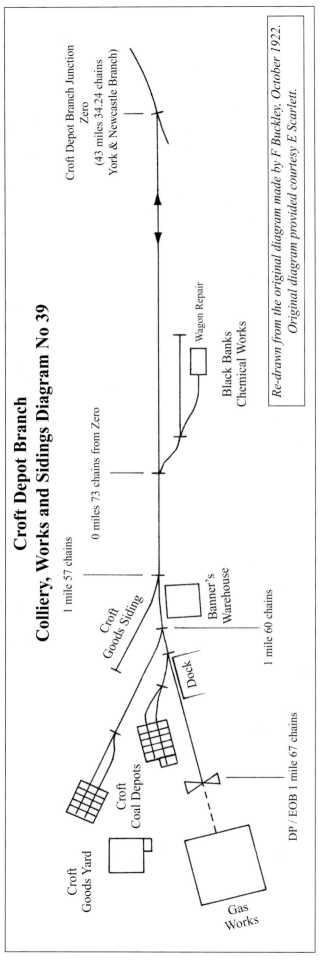

Croft Depot Branch
Colliery, Works and Sidings Diagram No 39

Croft Depot Branch Junction
Zero
(43 miles 34.24 chains
York & Newcastle Branch)

Wagon Repair

Black Banks
Chemical Works

0 miles 73 chains from Zero

1 mile 57 chains

Croft
Goods Siding

Banner's
Warehouse

Dock

1 mile 60 chains

Croft
Coal Depots

Croft
Goods Yard

DP / EOB 1 mile 67 chains

Gas
Works

Re-drawn from the original diagram made by F Buckley, October 1922.
Original diagram provided courtesy E Scarlett.

34

On 20 October 1829, shortly prior to the opening of the Croft Depot Branch, the S&DR's secretary issued a notice informing the public that coals from eight separate collieries would be available from the day of opening. That implies at least eight separate coal cells, and the remains of some of them are included in this view (left, taken on 1 May 1964).

The Durham Chronicle in June 1830 stated that there were at that time 22 cells in use. The additional cells were built on an extension to the easternmost sidings serving the original cells; the photographer is standing upon them to take this photograph. (RV Webster)

1 May 1964, and a view along the long line of coal cells built to augment the original ones (which have long been out of use by this date). The cells were served by two tracks, allowing a significant tonnage of coal to be deposited in each cell. To the right of the two tracks was a third, seen here cut back, that formerly served the gasworks. (RV Webster)

Another photograph taken on 1 May 1964: a view of the long line of coal cells as observed from the depot yard. (RV Webster)

In due course, the branch was re-aligned at its north end, and it became part of the north - south main line. The southern portion of the branch was unaffected. Coal continued to be conveyed to Croft Depot, though initially at least in lesser tonnages than hitherto. Indeed, traffic fell further when the Richmond Branch was opened in 1846. The local coal traffic remained though, and this gradually built up over the years, especially after a gasworks was built at Hurworth Place; some of the long line of coal cells were demolished to make way for it. The year of the establishment of the gas works is thought to have been 1858 as The Durham Chronicle reported that the second ordinary general meeting of the Croft &

Hurworth Gas Company was held on 31 January 1859.

It is not known when, but at some time merchandise traffic began to be conveyed to Croft Depot, and traffic was also generated from a private siding halfway along the branch. At the time of the survey for the 1857 OS map, the siding was used by the Black Banks Brick and Tile Works. When this works closed (date unknown) the site was occupied by the Black Banks Chemical Works (marked as 'Blackbanks' on the 1899, 1923 and 1948 OS maps).

Traffic levels were always relatively modest, however, and the Croft Depot Branch remained something of a quiet backwater until British Railways closed it on Monday, 27 April 1964.(30)

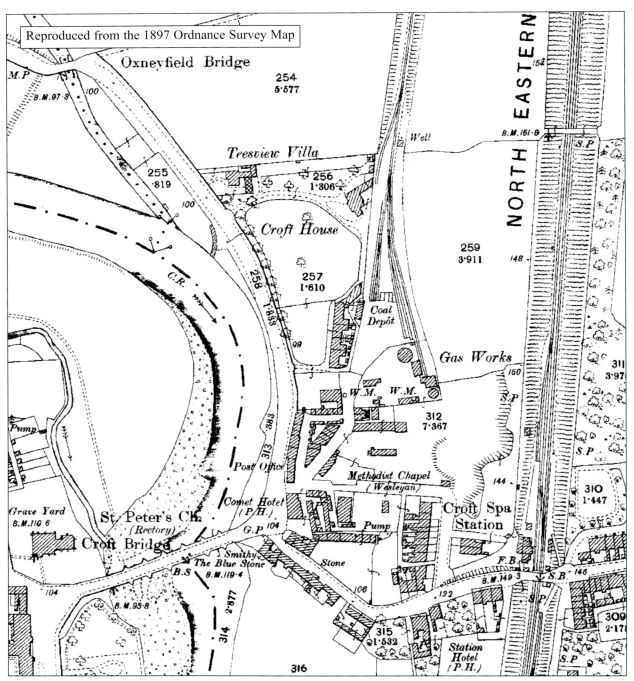

Croft Depot weigh house, 1 May 1964; the Morris Minor Traveller is parked just short of the weighbridge. The building may also have served as the residence of the S&DR's agent, George Langstaff, who was appointed when the branch first opened for traffic. (RV Webster)

Train Operation on the Croft Depot Branch

The S&DR's 3½ miles long Croft Depot Branch was single track. Traffic was originally horse-drawn, and it is likely that to allow trains going in opposite directions to pass there were passing places as was the case on the S&DR's main line. Passing places were not signalled, and drivers stayed on the running line or took the passing siding according to a defined set of priorities; loaded trains took precedence over empty trains, for example.

It is not known how the GNER signalled the branch. The signalling arrangements put in place by the North Eastern were recorded in *Appendix A to the General Rules and Regulations and to the Working Time Table*, in effect from 1 January 1898.

Single Lines over which Passenger Trains DO NOT run are worked as indicated.		
Line	Worked by	Staff kept in charge of
Croft Junction to Croft Depots	Round brass staff	Signalman at Croft Junction Box

By 1 March 1922, and the issue of a revised *Appendix*, the round brass staff was in charge of the Yard Inspector at Croft Junction.

No 65860 has arrived at Croft Depot and propels the four loaded coal wagons on to the long line of coal cells. In the upper photograph can be seen two 12 ton van bodies mounted on concrete blocks which correspond to 'Banner's Warehouse' as shown on Colliery, Works and Sidings Diagram No 39. (Both photographs : NT Coulthard)

The LNER's Working Time Table in effect 8 April to 7 July 1929 shows that at that time the branch was worked by Pilot Trains working from Croft Junction Goods Yard and from the goods station at Darlington North Road. Each working day except Monday, at 5:15 am a Pilot Train departed Croft Junction Goods Yard to serve Black Banks Chemical Works only. (Departure was 15 minutes later on a Monday.) Also each working day, a Pilot Train departed North Road at 10:30 am; this called at Croft Junction Goods Yard, the chemical works and Croft Depot. It was timetabled to start working home from Croft Depot at 1:25 pm.

British Railways' *Working of Local Engines : Darlington District*, in effect from 3 November 1952, shows that by this date the Croft Depot Branch was served by only one train per day, the 2:45 pm from Croft Yard.

Class J94 No 68060 shunts Croft Depot. There are two vans in the short train, and nearest the locomotive is a 13 ton mineral wagon. (DR Wilcock Collection)

This 1960s view of the original coal cells at Croft Depot shows that although they have not been rail served for many years, one at least is being used to store coal; presumably this is an overflow from one of the long line of coal cells. (DR Wilcock Collection)

Adjacent to the two van bodies mounted on concrete blocks was this platelayers' hut, roughly constructed from old sleepers and corrugated iron sheets. The photograph was taken on 1 May 1964. (RV Webster)

Right : Class J94 No 68060 shunts the sidings at Black Banks Chemical Works; wagons have been left on the single-track Croft Depot Branch while the shunting takes place. The lack of a run-round loop here meant that wagons had to be propelled back up the branch to Darlington and could not be accommodated in the routine pick-up working down to Croft Depot. (DR Wilcock Collection)

Below : There were two sidings at the chemical works. A short one ended beneath the corrugated iron shed seen in the background in both photographs. A longer siding passed beneath the timber loading gantry seen here. It looks as though solid blocks of pitch are being loaded into hopper wagons. (DR Wilcock Collection)

Left : Another view of Class J94 No 68060 shunting the chemical works. (DR Wilcock Collection)

Below : This photograph was taken on an overcast 28 May 1961. Modern cylindrical tank wagons are seen in the sidings at the Black Banks Chemical Works, in contrast to the antiquated rectangular ones seen below. (NERA KL Taylor Collection, per DR Wilcock)

Left : These 14 ton tar wagons, photographed in 1960 at Darlington Gas Works where they loaded the by-products of gas production, were operated by Thomas Ness Limited which owned the Black Banks Chemical Works. Thomas Ness wagon No 85 (on the left here) was built in January 1912 by Charles Roberts, Wakefield, and registered by the NER as No 8258. Thomas Ness wagon No 105 (on the right) was built in September 1913 by Hurst Nelson, Motherwell, and registered by the NER as No 8571. (RV Webster)

The Forcett Railway

Heinrich Wilhelm Ferdinand Bölckow was born in 1806, in Sülten, Mecklenburg. As a young man he made passage across the German Ocean to Newcastle upon Tyne where he built up a fortune as a corn merchant. Through his future wife, he met and became very friendly with John Vaughan, the manager of an ironworks at Walker. The two men decided to go into partnership as ironmasters, and to that end bought land from Joseph Pease in Middlesbrough in order to found an ironworks. Middlesbrough was developing industrially since the arrival of the Stockton & Darlington Railway, and both the railway and the River Tees offered economical transport for raw materials in and for finished goods out. Bolckow, Vaughan & Company's Vulcan Street Iron Works opened for business in August 1841. (Note the dropping of the umlaut from Bolckow's surname.)

The required pig iron was initially imported from Scotland, but in 1846 the company built blast furnaces at Witton Park (about 20 miles north-west of Middlesbrough, and a few miles west of Bishop Auckland) where there was a plentiful supply of coal and coke and where it was hoped that the iron ore found in the coal measures could be exploited. The latter did not happen. The company had instead to obtain ore from mines around Grosmont, which was shipped from Whitby to Middlesbrough, and from there conveyed by rail to Witton Park. Limestone also came in by rail, from Weardale. (The limestone was used as a flux in the blast furnaces, wherein it combined with the impurities released when smelting the iron ore.) The first pig iron to be produced at Witton Park was tapped from the furnace on 14 February 1846. This pig iron was then conveyed by rail to the Vulcan Street Iron Works.

The costs associated with transporting iron ore from Grosmont to Witton Park, and then pig iron from Witton Park to the works in Middlesbrough, were considerable. So Vaughan and his surveyor, John Marley, sought a more convenient supply. Given that over the years iron ore had been found in various places in the Cleveland Hills, the two men were no doubt optimistic; they made the required discovery in the Eston Hills in June 1850. The company therefore leased mining rights and in September the first trial load of ore was despatched to Witton Park. The trial was deemed a success – the ore typically yielding about 28% iron – and mining then began in earnest.

Significant quantities of ore were extracted, so much so that in 1851 the company built blast furnaces at the Middlesbrough works, and, in 1853, at a new site near Eston. (The furnaces at Witton Park remained in blast. Indeed, they were extended, finally closing in 1884.) Messrs Bolckow and Vaughan were not the only iron masters at work on Teesside; by 1855, there were 30 blast furnaces at work within 6 miles of Middlesbrough.

THE FORCETT RAILWAY COMPANY.

No. 1654   £20. SHARE.

This is to certify that JOHN EDWARD MAC NAY, Darlington, is the Proprietor of the Share Numbered 1654 in the FORCETT RAILWAY COMPANY, subject to the Rules, Regulations, and Orders of the said Company.

Given under the Common Seal of the said Company. Dated the 13 April in the year of our Lord one Thousand Eight hundred and 76

Secretary.

Forcett Railway Company share number 1654, as issued to John Edward MacNay. MacNay was secretary both to the Forcett Limestone Company and to the Darlington Section of the North Eastern Railway, i.e. the former Stockton & Darlington Railway. (MJ Denholm Collection)

The enormous expansion in the number of blast furnaces on Teesside vastly increased the tonnages of iron ore processed, which increased the competition between the various ironmasters for the available markets. An ironmaster's competitive edge being sharpened by a reduction in costs, there was pressure to find, for example, a more convenient supply of limestone than that obtained from Weardale. This was a particular necessity for those blast furnaces charged with Eston ore, as its siliceous nature meant that much more limestone flux was required compared with coal measures ore. For many years past, carboniferous limestone had been quarried to the west of Darlington around the village of Forcett for local building and agricultural purposes. Since 1856, when the Darlington & Barnard Castle Railway had been opened, this area was potentially accessible by rail. Given that the area was closer to Teesside than were the quarries in Weardale, the directors of the Stockton & Darlington Railway – which worked the Darlington & Barnard Castle – contemplated a branch off it to Forcett. But the money was not forthcoming, and no branch was built.

However, in 1864, Bolckow, Vaughan and others promoted the construction of such a railway which was to be built by themselves but operated by the Darlington Section of the North Eastern Railway (*i.e.* the former Stockton & Darlington, which had amalgamated with the North Eastern the previous year). The promotion, supported by the Forcett Limestone Company Limited, which planned to despatch per annum some 200,000 tons of limestone, was brought to a successful conclusion; an Act of Parliament incorporating the Forcett Railway Company was granted Royal Assent on 2 June 1865.(31) The Act named the new company's directors, amongst whom were Henry Bolckow (soon replaced by his nephew and eventual heir, Carl FH Bolckow), John Vaughan's son Thomas and Major Thomas Light Elwon of the South Bank Iron Works.

Construction of the five miles long Forcett Railway was to the plans of William Bryson, a Darlington-based civil engineer. To pay for that construction, the Act authorised the raising of £30,000 in the form of 1500 shares of £20 each; a further £10,000 could be borrowed on mortgage once all of the shares had been taken up and half of the capital actually paid. Construction began on 27 July 1865 when the daughter of the Lord of the Manor of Forcett, Miss Michell, cut the first sod with a ceremonial spade and deposited it in a ceremonial wheel barrow.(32) Having done her bit, Miss Michell handed over the rest of the construction task to the navvies employed by the contractor, Messrs Trowsdale & Son of Stockton.

John Trowsdale had been awarded the contract on the basis of his having put in the lowest bid: £19,680. As was often the case with such affairs, the contract had been awarded on price alone, with little consideration as to whether it was adequate for the task. In due course, Trowsdale discovered that he had quoted far too low a price, and began to suffer financial difficulties. These manifested themselves in slow progress in the works, and during the meeting of the Forcett Railway Company board held on 2 November 1865, it was minuted that directors were 'very much dissatisfied

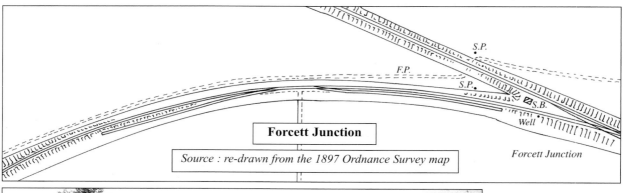

Forcett Junction

Source : re-drawn from the 1897 Ordnance Survey map

Forcett Junction on 16 October 1966, looking west. The Forcett Branch bears away to the left. Note the lack of track beyond the junction, this stretch of the Darlington & Barnard Castle Branch having closed on 5 April 1965. (RV Webster)

with slow progress of the works'. In December 1865, navvies complained to the board that the provisions of the Truck Act were not being observed. Trowsdale promised that nothing of the kind would happen again.

In May 1866, a board member was deputed to ask the promoters of the Merrybent Railway, which would run more or less parallel to the Forcett Railway some miles to the east, to abandon their proposed line. If the Merrybent was constructed instead as an extension to the Forcett Railway, some £40,000 would be saved. The appeal fell on deaf ears, and in due course the Merrybent & Darlington Railway would be constructed as an independent concern.

Meanwhile, back on the Forcett Railway, Trowsdale was struggling to pay his men. He asked the board to extend him payments even before the work to which they applied was completed. The board agreed to make such payments, but only if they were used to pay wages. This meant that Trowsdale could not afford to hire a locomotive when he deemed that he needed one. The board hired one instead, from Harris & Company, and loaned it to Trowsdale. In July 1866, Trowsdale went bankrupt; the Forcett Railway Company took over his plant, employed his navvies directly, and continued with the task of constructing of the line.

In December 1866 the board was asked by the Forcett Limestone Company if a few tons of limestone could be despatched over it. The board agreed to the quarrymen's request; charges would be calculated at a later date.

The navvies more or less completed their task in February 1867, and in that month the directors declared the railway open for traffic. However, it was not yet in a fit condition for the North Eastern to work locomotives over it. The first trains of limestone to be worked over the Forcett Railway were therefore hauled by the quarry company's locomotives to Piercebridge station where they were handed over to the North Eastern.(33)

In May 1867, Alfred O Walker was engaged to erect an electric telegraph to serve the railway; the two wires of the telegraph would operate double needle instruments, and trains would operate under the authority of a train staff. Walker was the Darlington Section's Telegraph Superintendent, having been appointed in 1865 to install the Block System of signalling between Middlesbrough and Darlington, and an electric telegraph serving the entire line.

Meanwhile, in order to cope with the anticipated heavy traffic off the Forcett Railway, the North Eastern had doubled the single-line Darlington & Barnard Castle Branch from Piercebridge westwards to the junction with the Forcett Railway.(34) As agreed with the promoters of the Forcett Railway, and as sanctioned by the Act, the North Eastern had also contracted to work goods traffic on that railway. However, an inspection by North Eastern directors and engineers in early June 1867 showed that not all the track was yet ballasted, and that earth slips were occurring in one of the cuttings. Until these faults were dealt with, the North Eastern still declined to work the traffic. This situation pertained until 17 June, when the North Eastern began to work the trains over the length of the Forcett Railway, providing locomotives, wagons and sheets as required. The Forcett Railway Company was responsible for track maintenance.

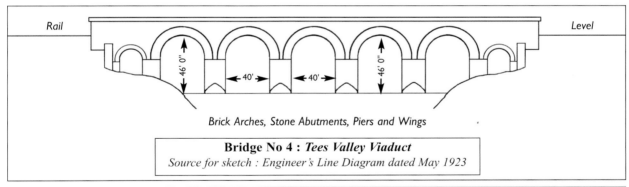

Rail   Level

46' 0"   40'   40'   46' 0"

Brick Arches, Stone Abutments, Piers and Wings

Bridge No 4 : *Tees Valley Viaduct*
Source for sketch : Engineer's Line Diagram dated May 1923

The bricks used to form the arches of the Tees Valley Viaduct were white firebricks, made at Messrs Chapman and Morson's Crook Colliery. The train crossing the viaduct comprises two sheeted open wagons and a brake van – a somewhat less well-loaded train than that seen on the front cover. (JW Armstrong / Armstrong Railway Photographic Trust)

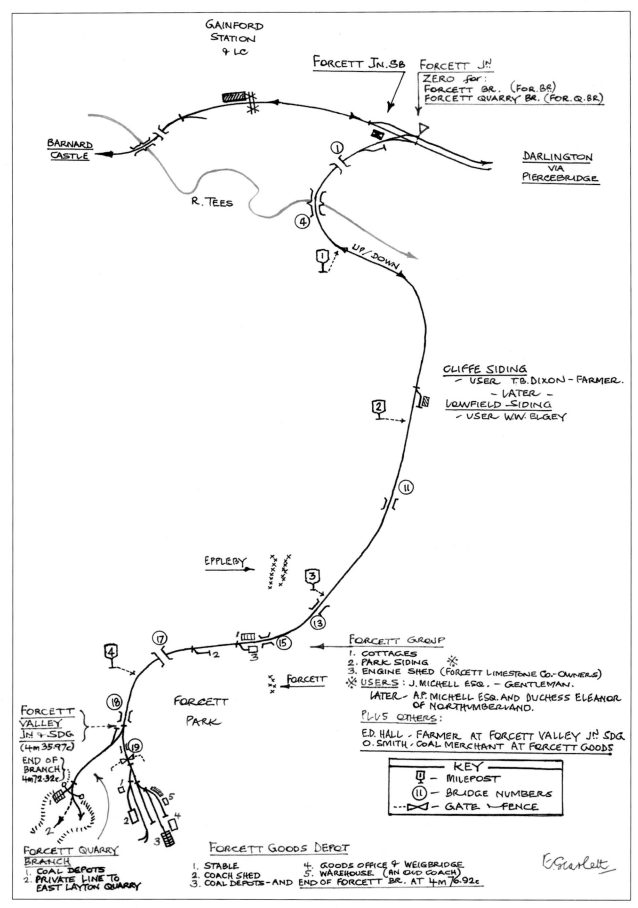

This diagram shows the locations of sidings etc. on the Forcett Railway, which became part of the LNER on 1 January 1923 upon the Grouping of the British railway companies. The Engineer's Line Diagram was drawn in May 1923, and all the siding diagrams that the NERA has in its archive were also drawn post-Grouping, in November 1924. (E Scarlett)

A Description of the Forcett Railway

From Forcett Junction, 6 miles 12 chains from the Darlington & Barnard Castle Branch zero point, the ruling gradient on the Forcett Railway was downhill to the River Tees, and uphill beyond; overall, these gradients were unfavourable for goods traffic bound for Forcett, but favourable for the heavy limestone trains travelling the other way – from Forcett Quarry to Forcett Junction.

During the lifetime of the Forcett Railway, existing sidings were extended as required and new ones laid in. The 1897 Ordnance Survey map shows two sidings at Forcett Junction, one trailing and the other facing for trains running on to the branch. Only the former was still in place to be recorded on the Engineer's Line Diagram dated May 1923: the 8 chains 8 yards Forcett Junction Siding. Beyond the siding the single-track railway curved south-west to a crossing of the River Tees via the 275 feet long, seven-arch Tees Valley Viaduct. Beyond the viaduct the railway curved south-eastwards and then south as it approached Cliffe (later Lowfield) Siding. This siding, 3 chains 9 yards long, served the local farmer (in 1898, Thomas Bellamy Dixon, farmer and land agent).(35)

Running approximately south south-west, the railway passed between the villages of Eppleby and Forcett, curving south-west to do so. In December 1868, the limestone company leased land from the railway company south-west of Eppleby near the Eppleby - Forcett road in order to build an engine shed and two cottages. The stone-built shed, at the end of the single-track 2 chains 9 yards Forcett Engine Shed Siding, accommodated the locomotives used to work wagons between the quarry and the exchange sidings at Forcett Goods Station. According to the 1881 Census, the cottages housed two families, the head of each of which was described as a locomotive man: George James, loco engine driver; William Robinson, loco fireman.(36)

Beyond the Eppleby - Forcett road, the railway ran in a large curve round the edge of Forcett Park – the parkland surrounding Forcett Hall, the seat of the Lord of the Manor and one of the North Riding's Deputy Lieutenants, John Michell. Forcett Park Siding, 3 chains 7 yards long, served the needs of the most important local landowners, the Michell family and the Duke of Northumberland.

Forcett Goods Station was at the end of the line, beyond which lay the rail-served quarry of the Forcett Limestone Company. This quarry was highly productive; in the early 1870s, it was busy enough to require the services of two quarry company locomotives.(37) At the goods station there were loading docks and coal cells for the accommodation of goods traffic other than limestone. In the 1890s, Marmaduke Webster served here as the North Eastern's goods and coal agent, and as the Forcett Limestone Company's clerk.(38) At some time a North Eastern Railway covered wagon was lifted off its wheels and placed in the station yard for use as a warehouse.(39)

Forcett Quarry Branch

Circa 1872, the Forcett Limestone Company decided to open new quarries a short distance to the west of those currently being worked. (In due course, and certainly by 1892, the original quarries would be abandoned.) To serve the new quarries, the railway company sought

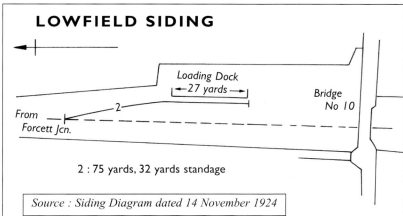

LOWFIELD SIDING

Loading Dock
← 27 yards →

Bridge No 10

From Forcett Jcn.

2 : 75 yards, 32 yards standage

Source : Siding Diagram dated 14 November 1924

— 17' 9" —
Brick Arch, Stone Abutments and Wings

Bridge No 10 : *Green Lane*
Accommodation Overbridge
*Source for sketch :
Engineer's Line Diagram*

Rail Level

— 18' 0" —
Brick Arch, Stone Abutments and Wings

Bridge No 15 : *Tank Bridge*
Underbridge, Forcett - Eppleby Road
*Source for sketch :
Engineer's Line Diagram*

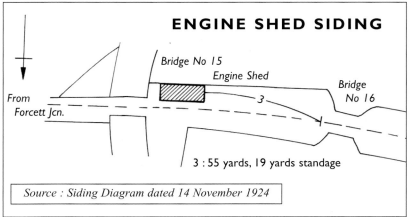

ENGINE SHED SIDING

Bridge No 15
Engine Shed

Bridge No 16

From Forcett Jcn.

3 : 55 yards, 19 yards standage

Source : Siding Diagram dated 14 November 1924

the sanction of the Board of Trade to raise additional capital so that a new branch could be constructed. The civil engineers Messrs Nimmo and MacNay were engaged to survey and plan the proposed branch, and the resulting plans, sections and book of reference were deposited with the Clerk of the Peace for the North Riding on 14 November 1872. This deposition was presumably made on the assumption that the sanction of the Board of Trade would be obtained in due course; on 25 March 1873 the Board duly issued a certificate allowing the company to raise an additional £4200 in share capital and £1400 in loans. However, no Act of Parliament for the branch has been found by the present authors. The land required for it was owned by John Michell, and it may have been the case that a private agreement was reached between him and the railway company, and that the sanction of Parliament was not in the end sought.

Robert Palmer was contracted to construct the Forcett Quarry Branch; work was completed in 1876. According to the deposited plans, it was 3 furlongs 6.7 chains long; it would be extended over the years as the working faces of the quarries were pushed deeper into the countryside. The branch diverged from the main line of the Forcett Railway at Forcett Valley Junction, situated on the western edge of Forcett Park. It is not clear when it was laid in, but a siding off the branch close to the junction, Forcett Valley Siding, was recorded in both 1898 and 1918 as being used by Edward Hall, a local farmer. Beyond junction and siding lay exchange sidings, coal cells and quarry company tracks to Forcett and East Layton Quarries.

Forcett Railway Extension

For most of its length, the Forcett Quarry Branch ran westwards. (It curved to the south at its far end.) The Forcett Railway Extension was intended to reach further westwards still. TF MacNay was engaged to make a survey, and the plans for the 2 miles 2 furlongs and 6 chains extension were deposited with the Clerk of the Peace on 30 November 1881. The extension was planned to diverge from the Forcett Quarry Branch at about the point where it began to curve to the south; it would run westwards, pass south of Hutton Fields and terminate in a quarry at Lane Head. Once again no Act of Parliament appears to have been obtained, but in this case no railway resulted either; the extension was never constructed.

Left and below : the Forcett Limestone Company's engine shed south-west of Eppleby on 20 November 1965. The original shed was stone-built, but as can be seen here it was subsequently given a brick extension. Note that the squared-off stones of the original doorway have been brought forward to form the new doorway. Note also the corrugated iron roof of the extension; it looks as though a hole has been roughly broken through to allow smoke to escape. (RV Webster)

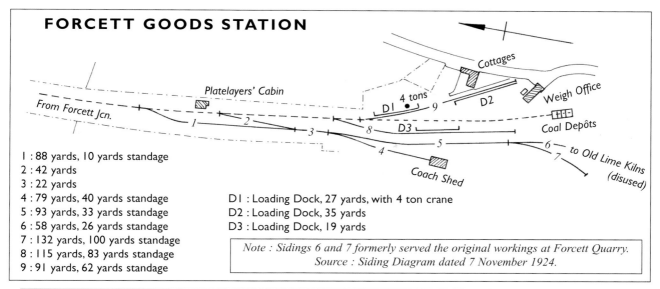

FORCETT GOODS STATION

From Forcett Jcn.

Platelayers' Cabin

Cottages

D1 • 4 tons

D2

Weigh Office

Coal Depôts

D3

Coach Shed

to Old Lime Kilns (disused)

1 : 88 yards, 10 yards standage
2 : 42 yards
3 : 22 yards
4 : 79 yards, 40 yards standage
5 : 93 yards, 33 yards standage
6 : 58 yards, 26 yards standage
7 : 132 yards, 100 yards standage
8 : 115 yards, 83 yards standage
9 : 91 yards, 62 yards standage

D1 : Loading Dock, 27 yards, with 4 ton crane
D2 : Loading Dock, 35 yards
D3 : Loading Dock, 19 yards

Note : Sidings 6 and 7 formerly served the original workings at Forcett Quarry.
Source : Siding Diagram dated 7 November 1924.

Two views of Forcett Goods Station, Saturday, 7 March 1964. Note the vans lifted off their wheels and in use as warehouses. The bogie passenger full brake vans in the centre of the top photograph, still on their wheels, are also in use as warehouses; they are both labelled 'STORAGE VAN NOT TO LEAVE FORCETT'.

The goods station was all but moribund by 1964. Typical figures for busier times were those for 1904 when Goods Forwarded totalled 2343 tons, principally comprising roadstone, barley, timber, potatoes, oats, wheat, hay and clover and livestock; Goods Received totalled 2883 tons. Coal was received too, but there is no entry in the records. Total receipts in 1904 were £684, included in which was £3 for 'Parcels, Horses, Carriages, Dogs &c.' Station expenses came to £125.

Tonnage of limestone despatched from the quarries was 162,224 in 1906, 168,932 in 1907 and 139,265 in 1908. (RB Coulthard)

Above : Forcett Goods Station, date not known. At the loading dock are an open wagon, a van and a cattle van. At the far side of the yard is a large van with two sets of doors, off its wheels and in use as a warehouse. In the left foreground is the weigh office and associated weighbridge. (Ken Hoole Study Centre Collection)

Left : After a disinfection of footwear – the site of Forcett Goods Station was in use as a chicken farm – this photograph was taken on 31 December 1991 of one of four van bodies still used for storage. It was built in 1903 as a 15 ton Diagram G4 Road Van. (DR Wilcock)

Right : The derelict coal cells at Forcett Goods, photographed on 16 October 1966. There is a glimpse to the right of another van body in use as a warehouse. (RV Webster)

The Forcett Limestone Company operated a number of locomotives over the years. This is 'East Layton', R&W Hawthorn, Leslie & Company Limited Works No 2871, bought new by the limestone company in 1911. It is seen at work here on 3 June 1940. NER traffic records show the following tonnages of limestone despatched from the quarries: 1913, 128,185 tons; 1914, 103,830 tons; 1920, 124,240 tons. (G Alliez / Ken Hoole Study Centre Collection)

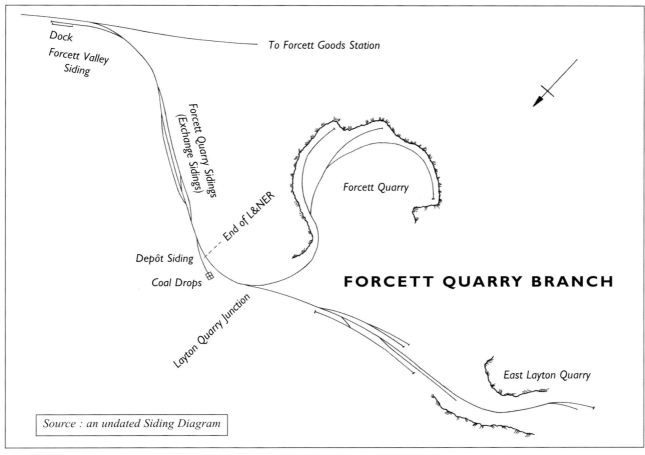

Dock

Forcett Valley Siding

To Forcett Goods Station

Forcett Quarry Sidings (Exchange Sidings)

Forcett Quarry

End of L&NER

Depôt Siding

Coal Drops

FORCETT QUARRY BRANCH

Layton Quarry Junction

East Layton Quarry

Source : an undated Siding Diagram

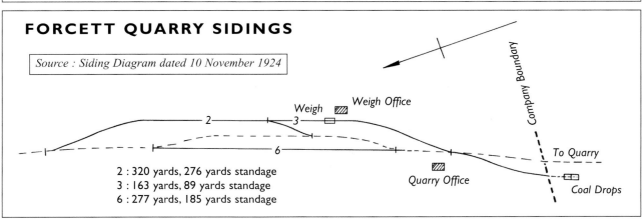

FORCETT QUARRY SIDINGS

Source : Siding Diagram dated 10 November 1924

Company Boundary

Weigh
Weigh Office

2

3

6

To Quarry

Quarry Office

Coal Drops

2 : 320 yards, 276 yards standage
3 : 163 yards, 89 yards standage
6 : 277 yards, 185 yards standage

Forcett Valley Junction, looking southwards to Forcett Goods Station on 7 March 1964. The Forcett Quarry Branch bears away to the right; Forcett Valley Siding is partially hidden under the snow. (RB Coulthard)

East Layton Estate Private Branch Railway

John Michell owned the land to the north of the westwards-running portion of the Forcett Quarry Branch. In 1878 he engaged Messrs RJ Semple and Wm Cockburn to plan a private railway at the western end of this land. The plans deposited with the Clerk of the Peace on 29 November 1878 do not show any railway tracks, merely an area some 15 chains east to west and 3 chains north to south in which they would be located. Perhaps a field railway of the Decauville type was intended, bringing stone to standard gauge wagons in a siding on the Forcett Quarry Branch. Nothing shows up on contemporary Ordnance Survey maps, so it is not clear what transpired – if anything ever did.

Hutton Magna Light Railway

In 1913, William Spencer, quarry owner and limestone merchant, promoted a standard gauge light railway that would branch off the Forcett Railway and run westwards to Hutton Magna. The intention was to exploit the limestone deposits around the village, both for steel-making and agricultural purposes. Sebastian William Meyer, who had made a name for himself with such as the Cawood, Wistow & Selby Light Railway, was engaged to make a survey. The resulting railway was planned to branch off the Forcett Railway where it passed above the north end of Forcett Park, curve north to Caldwell Mill, curve back south again and then run westwards, passing south of Little Hutton and between West Middleton and Hutton Magna. Beyond the village of Hutton Magna the railway would curve to the south and terminate; planned length was 3 miles 3 furlongs and 8 chains. Meyer estimated the cost of land, construction and buildings at £17,356. Rolling stock would cost £3000. Including diverse sundries, total cost would be £22,356.

The railway was to be constructed under the provisions of the Light Railways Act, 1896. Plans, sections and book of reference were deposited with the Clerk of the Peace on 27 November 1913. The Light Railway Commissioners held a public enquiry into the proposed railway at the King's Head Hotel, Barnard Castle, on 14 February 1914. This went well for Spencer and Meyer, and Commissioners subsequently approved a Draft Order, confirmed by the Board of Trade on 17 May 1915. The newly-authorised light railway company was permitted to raise £24,000 by way of 2400 £100 shares, and to borrow £8000. It had always been intended that goods and minerals would conveyed, but the Light Railway Order obtained also permitted passengers to be carried. However, all these efforts would be in vain; the light railway would never be constructed.

Passenger Train Operation on the Forcett Railway

The Forcett Railway Company's Act of Parliament included clauses specifying the maximum fares chargeable for passenger traffic, and for such as how much luggage each class of passenger was permitted to carry free of charge. In December 1884, the company bought from the North Eastern for £35 No 179, a four-wheeled Third Class carriage that had been built by the Stockton & Darlington Railway in 1865.(40) This was housed in a shed erected at Forcett Goods Station. The presumption must be that this, hauled by a quarry company locomotive, was used to convey quarrymen between their homes in the villages of Eppleby and Forcett and the quarries, though details are not known. The carriage has survived, and is now at Beamish - Living Museum of the North.

FATAL ACCIDENT NEAR RICHMOND.- An inquiry into the death of Robert Wappett, who was killed on the previous evening, was held at Forcett, at ten o'clock on Thursday evening last, before Mr. Walton, coroner. It appears that deceased was a fireman employed on a tank engine at Forcett Limestone Quarry, but on Wednesday evening he and his mate were engaged running some people from the Gainford Horse and Foal Show. Deceased accidentally fell across the line, and the engine passed over him, taking both his legs off below the knee, and he expired almost immediately. A verdict of "Accidental Death" was returned. Deceased was twenty-one years of age and resided with his parents at Forcett Valley.

This clipping is from 'The Northern Echo' dated 10 August 1874. The NER had a station at Gainford, but there is no reason to suppose that the Forcett train ran there. It is likely to have run on Forcett Railway metals as far as the Darlington - Barnard Castle road; the passengers will have walked to the show via the road. Note that this tragic accident occurred before the company bought the former S&DR carriage from the North Eastern. (NERA KP Plant Collection)

Mineral Train Operation on the Forcett Railway

Although it had always been intended that the Forcett Railway be worked by the North Eastern, the Act that sanctioned its construction did of course include the usual clauses concerning maximum tolls to be charged for diverse classes of goods traffic. The main intended traffic, limestone, was to be charged at a maximum toll of one penny per ton per mile if it was conveyed in North Eastern wagons; in the unlikely event that the Forcett Railway Company was to provide its own wagons, an additional farthing per ton per mile could be charged. How the receipts were to be divided between the two companies was subject to a separate agreement. From the total receipts from limestone traffic, the North Eastern's accountant allocated each company tuppence per ton; the balance of the receipts was then divided in proportion to the mileage travelled over each company's metals. However, from the payments due to the Forcett Railway Company, the North Eastern retained 30% to cover the cost of working the traffic.

The division of receipts was to the same principle for other mineral and goods traffic.

When the Forcett Railway opened fully in 1867, the Darlington & Barnard Castle Branch was still largely single track. This led to extensive discussions within the North Eastern as to how trains were to be run to and from the Forcett Railway. There was a strong body of opinion that the best way to proceed would be to make Piercebridge a regular single-line staff station; however, for reasons unknown William Bouch objected to this. After much discussion, in March 1869 the working arrangements were agreed; see the notice reproduced above.(41)

If the traffic on offer required an afternoon Forcett mineral train, then its working would again have to mesh with the existing traffic on the Darlington & Barnard Castle.

In order to regulate the traffic on to and off the Forcett Railway, the North Eastern determined that a signal would be required at the junction. Accordingly, on 16 July 1869 a letter was written to the Forcett board stating that the cost of a signal, signal box *etc.* would be

---

NORTH EASTERN RAILWAY.

DARLINGTON SECTION.

FORCETT MINERAL TRAINS.

NOTICE.

The **FORCETT** Train is to start from Darlington at 5-50 a.m. and precede No. 4 Up Train which leaves at 6-0 a.m., and take a Ticket to Piercebridge and leave it there.

No. **10 UP GOODS and MINERAL** Train now leaving Darlington at 10-10 a.m. will leave at 9-45 a.m., taking the Staff and leaving it at Piercebridge Station, and receive the Ticket left at Piercebridge by the FORCETT TRAIN, and take it to Barnard Castle, and leave it there.

N.B. The Station Master at Piercebridge will be held responsible for the Ticket being left by the Forcett Train, and handed to No. 10 Up Train at Piercebridge.

The **FORCETT** Train must return from Piercebridge at 10-0 a.m., or as soon as the Staff arrives from Darlington, and bring the Staff to Darlington in time for the No. 13 Up Passenger Train at 10-35.

The above arrangement to come into operation on Monday, March 22nd, 1869.

BY ORDER.

DARLINGTON, *March 18th*, 1869.

(NER / NERA KP Plant Collection)

---

about £386. The North Eastern proposed that the Forcett Railway pay £200 towards this cost, plus half the wages of the signalman. The Forcett board did not think a signal necessary, but eventually agreed to pay £150, plus half the signalman's wages.

On 1 June 1870, the Merrybent & Darlington Railway – built essentially for the same purpose as the Forcett Railway – was opened a few miles to the east. This new railway also made a junction with the Darlington & Barnard Castle Branch, and to cope with the additional traffic the North Eastern had doubled it from Darlington (Hopetown Junction) to Piercebridge.(42) The Darlington & Barnard Castle Branch was now double track from Darlington to Forcett Junction, necessitating the use of single-line train staffs only by trains running beyond the junction to Barnard Castle.

In April 1870, Colonel CS Hutchinson, serving as a Board of Trade Inspecting Officer, had visited

Merrybent Junction in order to inspect it and to determine if the working arrangements were such that it could be safely opened for traffic. During the course of his inspection he had observed that the line had been doubled from Darlington to Forcett Junction, but in violation of the 1842 Regulation of Railways Act the new works had not been submitted for inspection. Hutchinson returned in early June 1870 and recorded that there were 'junctions provided with locking apparatus' at Hopetown, Staff [later named Stooperdale], Merrybent and Forcett, 'the first being that of the main line from Bishop Auckland and the other three those of mineral lines'.(43)

The North Eastern's Northern Division Working Time Table effective from 1 September 1870 showed the effects wrought by the introduction of double track as far as Forcett Junction. The Forcett mineral train (Train No 9) now left Darlington at 7:25 am, and Train No 10, the Up goods and mineral, left Darlington at 8:15 am. The afternoon Forcett mineral, Train No 18, departed Darlington at 3 pm.

The single-line Forcett Railway was also worked by train staff, as a single section. In February 1871 it was decided that there should henceforth be two sections; these were deemed necessary as the quarry company locomotives had to travel daily between the quarry and the engine shed. The two sections were: Forcett Junction - Eppleby (staff with one ring); Eppleby - Forcett (staff with two rings).(44)

At the beginning of 1892, the NER prepared a statement showing the weight of traffic, destination and division of revenues between the company and the Forcett Railway Company for the previous year. From Forcett Quarry, 191,562 tons 13 cwt of limestone were despatched to a total of 13 ironworks and foundries on Teesside. The receipts were divided £13,783 19s 7d to the NER and £4,110 2s 11d to the Forcett Railway Company. Coal, mostly household (1,889 tons 7 cwt) but some for use in the quarry (286 tons 7 cwt), and coke (116 tons 7 cwt) was conveyed to Forcett Goods and to the quarry. This traffic earned £252 10s 8d for the NER and £129 8s 2d for the Forcett Railway Company. However, 30% of the latter's revenues was extracted by the NER to cover working expenses. For the year 1891, total revenue earned by the NER was therefore £15,308 7s 7d; by the Forcett Railway Company £2,967 13s 9d.(45)

By 1898, the situation as regards the working of trains was as follows:(46; see also the illustrations inside the front cover.)

Single Lines over which Passenger Trains DO NOT run are worked as indicated.

Line	Worked by	Staff kept in charge of
1. Forcett Junction and Eppleby.	Brass staff with square handle and ticket.	Signalman at Forcett Junction or quarrymen at Eppleby.
2. Eppleby and New Quarry Office.	Brass staff with round handle and ticket.	Quarrymen at Eppleby or clerk at New Quarry Office.

Additional Regulations
Forcett Branch

1.—Drivers of engines or trains requiring to travel from the New Quarry to the Old Quarry or Goods Yard must in all cases be in possession of the Eppleby and New Quarry staff.

2.—The Forcett Quarry Company will arrange for a man being in attendance at Eppleby on the arrival and departure of all engines or trains, and who will have charge of the staffs and tickets there.

3.—The Forcett Company's Clerk, stationed at the New Quarry office will have charge of the staff and ticket working at that place.

4.—When it is necessary for the staff to be sent from the Quarries to Eppleby for an incoming train, care must be taken to see that this is done before the inward train leaves Forcett Junction.

5.—It must be understood that trains travelling to and from the Quarries shall not approach the Eppleby Engine Shed from opposite directions at the same time, also that engines must not foul the engine shed line until the driver is in possession of either the train staff or a train staff ticket.

6.—The person handing a staff to a driver must inform him whether an engine or train has preceded him, when the driver has a ticket he will know that no train has preceded him.

The same publication showed under Loads of Mineral Engines:
From Forcett Junction to Forcett Quarry   . . 30 empty wagons.
From Forcett Quarry to Darlington   . . . . 30 loaded wagons.

The volume of limestone traffic was such that the Working Time Table effective from 1 October 1897 included four Forcett mineral trains each weekday (departing Darlington North Road at 6:5 am, 9:5 am, 12:5 pm and 3:20 pm). However, these were all marked Q – 'runs as required' – and may not have run every day. Return trips from Forcett were timetabled for 7:55 am, 10:55 am, 1:55 pm and 5:15 pm. The 7:55 am arrived back at North Road at 8:35; at 9:10 it departed for South Bank, stopping as required at Stockton South Goods and Middlesbrough. The next two departures were also bound for South Bank, but the last of the day terminated at Cargo Fleet. Empties were worked back to North Road by the 11:30 am Forcett Mineral from South Bank (a train that was booked to run every weekday – unless the **Q** was omitted from the timetable in error) which picked up more empties at Newport, the 2:15 pm Forcett Mineral from South Bank (**Q**) which also picked up more empties at Newport, the 5:15 pm Forcett Mineral from South Bank (**Q**) which picked up more empties at Middlesbrough, and the 9 pm Forcett Mineral from South Bank (**Q**) which also picked up more empties at Newport.

Over time, production of steel became more important than that of iron. Sheffield gained an early lead in the production of steel, and it seemed for a time as though the iron industry on Teesside would disappear as quickly as it had arisen. The major problem on Teesside was that the Eston ore, typically containing 0.55% phosphorus, could not be utilised to make steel by the current methods. To get over this problem, Bolckow, Vaughan imported suitable haematite ore from Cumberland and Spain; this was smelted in a new steel-making plant built at Eston in 1876. As well as buying mines in Spain to keep the plant supplied, Bolckow, Vaughan employed two chemists to seek out a means of using the local Eston ore to make steel. These men gave their name to the Gilchrist-Thomas process, developed by them in 1879, which removed the phosphorus from the molten Eston pig-iron and allowed steel to be made from it. The new process gave back to Teesside its competitive edge, and more steel-making plants were built by Bolckow, Vaughan and others.

The most important product of the Teesside iron industry was iron rails, sold to railway administrations both at home and overseas. In 1872, 299,000 tons of iron rails were made on Teesside, comprising 48% of the tonnage of the Teesside manufactured iron.(47) The introduction of steel rails had a dramatic effect, as such rails typically lasted three times as long as the iron rails they replaced. By 1879, only 7000 tons of iron rails were made on Teesside, a mere 3% of the tonnage of manufactured iron. Manufacture of rails on Teesside was replaced by that of plates, bars and angles, a large proportion of which were used by the local

shipbuilding industry. Overall production of iron fell, though it was more than made up for by the production of steel; in 1910 681,593 tons of manufactured steel were produced on Teesside (and 168,208 tons of manufactured iron).

The basic requirement for limestone flux therefore remained, but over time the required tonnages reduced as more and more foreign ore was imported. (As related above, the highly siliceous Eston ore required the use of large quantities of limestone.) Local production of Eston ore peaked in 1885 with the mining of more than 6 million tons; even in 1885, 349,868 tons of foreign ore were imported into Teesside.(48) Tonnages of imported ore steadily increased as local production declined; in 1900, 1,250,840 tons of foreign ore were imported. The reducing demand for limestone flux inevitably affected traffic on the Forcett Railway.

The North Eastern's Working Time Table in force between July and September 1913 included only two Forcett mineral trains each working day: Train No 34, the Mondays excepted 8:5 am Class C Mineral North Road to Forcett or Train No 39, the Mondays only 9:5 am Class C Mineral North Road to Forcett; Train No 53, the 12:55 pm (Q) Class C Mineral North Road to Forcett.

Absorption into the LNER

On 1 January 1923, the British railway companies were compelled to merge by Act of Parliament into four large companies. The Forcett Railway Company would be absorbed by the London & North Eastern Railway. It had been a profitable company, regularly paying a dividend to its shareholders. From 1901 to 1913, it had paid an annual dividend of 5%.(49) In order to absorb the Forcett Railway Company, the LNER agreed to pay £34,200 in cash. (The Company was to retain its cash reserve of about £12,000.) Absorption was to take effect on 1 January 1923, with the payment of the £34,200 (plus interest, if after 1 January) to be made by 31 March 1923.

The London & North Eastern's Working Time Table effective from 8 April 1929 also included two Class C mineral trains each weekday, departing Darlington at 8:5 am bound for Forcett, arriving 9:4, and 12:45 pm bound for Forcett Quarry, arriving 1:29. The different

On 4 August 1964, having departed Forcett Goods, No 43050 shunts ballast hoppers in the Forcett Quarry Branch exchange sidings. Loaded wagons will be drawn off the branch to be added to the train left on the Forcett Branch. The completed train will then be conveyed to Darlington. (C Nettleton)

destinations of these two mineral trains seems to indicate how ordinary goods traffic was worked over the Forcett Railway. Of the two trains, only the one in the morning appears to have been booked to go to Forcett goods, and presumably it conveyed the ordinary goods traffic. On Mondays only, this departed Forcett at 11:9 for Forcett Quarry exchange sidings. Booked departure time from the sidings was 11:29. Mondays must have been busy at Forcett, as Mondays excepted the departure time from Forcett was 10:9 instead of 11:9.

On 4 September 1929, Superintendent CM Jenkin Jones issued revised instructions (O.2146) for working the traffic on the Forcett Branch:

Forcett Branch

Instructions for the working of trains between Forcett Junction, New Quarry and Forcett Goods Station.
(Taking the place of instructions in Circular T.S. 29 and T.S. 29A, dated December, 1897)

1.—This line is worked in accordance with the Regulations for Working Single Lines of Railway over which Passenger Trains do not run by Train Staff and one Train Staff Ticket, and the Signalman at Forcett Junction must regulate the running of trains on the branch by means of the telephone.

2.—The Forcett Junction Signalman must advise the Clerk at the New Quarry and the Forcett Goods Agent by telephone when a train leaves Forcett Junction, giving a description of the train.

Before the Quarry Company's engine leaves Eppleby Engine Shed for the New Quarry, the Driver must communicate with the Signalman at Forcett Junction by telephone and ascertain whether he must take the Ticket or Staff for the Eppleby New Quarry and Forcett Goods Section.

Before a train is allowed to leave the New Quarry or Forcett Goods Station for Forcett Junction the Quarry Clerk or Goods Agent, as the case may be, must advise the Forcett Junction Signalman the time the train will be ready to leave and obtain his permission for it to do so.

The Clerk at the New Quarry Office must advise the Signalman at Forcett Junction by telephone shortly before the Quarry Company's engine leaves the Quarry sidings for Eppleby Engine Shed, Forcett Goods Station or Forcett Park Siding, stating the time the engine will leave and its subsequent movements.

3.—Trains or engines must not be allowed to approach Eppleby from opposite directions at the same time, and the Signalman at Forcett Junction must arrange the working so that this is not possible.

By the time that the Working Timetable in effect from 4 July to 25 September 1938 was issued, stone traffic had declined to such an extent that the traffic to and from both Barton (on the former Merrybent & Darlington Railway) and Forcett Quarry were being dealt with by the same train; Train No 38, the 9:15 am Class C Goods from North Road West Sidings to Barton and Forcett Quarry. The return working was Train No 43, the Class C Goods to North Road East Yard; no timings were given in the timetable for this train. The Working Timetable in effect from 25 September 1939 to 28 April 1940 shows a similar Class C Goods, departing from North Road West Sidings at 8.45 am, again with no timings for the return working. Part of the reduction in traffic seems to have been because significant quantities of limestone for the Teesside steelworks were coming from Wensleydale – an average of 3700 tons per week circa 1938 – and local quarries at Aycliffe and Cornforth. Forcett, East Layton and Barton Quarries were providing Teesside with a total of 2850 tons per week.

Entries in the Fighting Cocks signal box Train Register Book for the months November and December 1942 show daily workings to Forcett Mondays to Saturdays. The westbound train passed the box between noon and 2 pm. The return working to Teesside usually passed the box between 4 and 6 pm, though occasionally it was nearer 8 pm and sometimes the passing was not recorded at all as the box only worked two shifts. In the latter case, presumably the train was routed via Geneva Junction and Dinsdale. The trains were signalled either '1 – 4' (unbraked goods or ballast) or '4 – 1' (mineral or empty wagons). Four locomotive numbers are recorded as working the trains: J25 locomotives numbers 1743, 2046, 2060 and 2140. Nos 2046 and 2140 were definitely allocated to Middlesbrough at this time, and it seems likely that the other two were also allocated to this shed.

The Final Years

On Teesside, steel production was concentrated in a few modern plants; Bolckow, Vaughan had been taken over in 1929 by Dorman, Long and Company Limited, which had built a new steel works at Redcar in 1917. The company built another new steel works at Lackenby in 1954. The demand for limestone flux was therefore sustained.

The goods traffic to Forcett Goods Station was, according to the Working Timetable effective from 19 September 1955, handled by train No 1738, the Class K pick-up goods departing Darlington (Albert Hill) at 9 am each morning. Calls at Forcett, however, were as required. The usual locomotive was an Ivatt 2MT 2-6-0 from Darlington shed.

On Sunday, 21 September 1958, in the face of declining overall rail traffic, the Darlington & Barnard Castle Branch was singled between Piercebridge and Forcett Junction in order to allow the closure of Forcett Junction signal box. This affected the way trains worked to and from the Forcett Branch. The closed signal box was replaced by a ground frame; appropriate new instructions (O.4317) were issued by Operating Officer L Sproat:

Piercebridge

Instructions for Working Forcett Junction Ground Frame

1. The Ground Frame consists of two levers, namely one points lever and one release lever as follows:—

    No. 1. Points, Main line—Branch line.

    No. 2. Lock on No. 1 points.

    No. 1 lever is released by No. 2 lever and No. 2 lever is released by Annetts Key and the Key Token for the Piercebridge - Winston Section.

2. An intermediate token instrument for the Piercebridge - Winston Section is provided in a hut alongside the Ground Frame in connection with which an indicator is installed which shows "locked" or "free".

3. Telephonic communication is provided between the hut alongside the Ground Frame and Piercebridge Signal Box.

4. When it is necessary to make use of the connection the Guard of the train concerned must act as follows:—

    (a) Trains requiring to enter the Forcett Branch.

        (i) Obtain the Key Token for the Piercebridge - Winston Section from the Driver, insert it in the left-hand lock on lever No. 2 and turn the key.

        (ii) Insert the Annetts Key, which is affixed to the Train Staff for the Forcett Junction - Eppleby Section, in the right-hand lock of lever No. 2 and turn the key.

        (iii) Reverse lever No. 2 and then reverse lever No. 1.

        (iv) Ensure the points are properly set for the safety of the train and then authorise the Driver to proceed on to the Forcett Branch.

        (v) After the train has passed clear on to the Branch, complete with tail lamp, return lever No. 1 to the normal position.

        (vi) Return lever No. 2 to the normal position, turn and withdraw the Annetts Key.

        (vii) Turn and withdraw the Key Token for the Piercebridge - Winston Section, place it in the intermediate token instrument and then give key a half-turn clockwise.

        (viii) Inform the Signalman at Piercebridge that the train is on the Forcett Branch clear of the main line, complete with tail lamp, the Ground Frame has been closed, the Key Token inserted in the intermediate token instrument and the track circuit indicator shows "clear". The guard must not leave the Ground Frame until he has received an assurance from the Signalman that everything is in order.

        (ix) Having received this assurance, hand the Train Staff for the Forcett Junction Ground Frame - Eppleby Section to the Driver and authorise him to proceed to Eppleby.

    (b) Trains requiring to leave the Forcett Branch for Piercebridge. (N.B.—It is not permissible to travel from the Forcett Branch direct to Winston.)

        (i) Obtain the Annetts Key from the Driver.

        (ii) Inform the Signalman at Piercebridge that the train is ready to proceed to Piercebridge and, when the Signalman gives the instruction, turn the Key Token as far as it will go (quarter-turn anti-clockwise) and when the indicator shows "free", make a further quarter-turn anti-clockwise and withdraw the Key Token for the Piercebridge - Winston Section from the intermediate token instrument.

        (iii) Place the Key Token in the left-hand lock on lever No. 2 and turn the key.

        (iv) Proceed as detailed in clauses (a) (ii) and (iii).

        (v) Ensure the points are properly set for the safety of the train and then authorise the Driver to proceed on to the main line clear of the points.

        (vi) After the train has passed dear on to the main line, complete with tail lamp, return lever No. 1 to the normal position.

        (vii) Return lever No. 2 to the normal position, turn and withdraw the Annetts Key and retain it until arrival at Piercebridge when it must be handed to the Signalman.

        (viii) Turn and withdraw the Key Token for the Piercebridge - Winston Section, hand the Key Token to the Driver and authorise him to proceed to Piercebridge.

5. In the event of a failure of equipment at the Ground Frame the Station Master, or other person in charge, must be informed at once and he must send for the Signal Engineer's representative appointed to attend such failures. Until the fault has been rectified use of the Ground Frame is prohibited, except in the case of a train being already on the Forcett Branch at the time of the failure.

    In such cases the Station Master must arrange to have the points disconnected by the Chief Civil Engineer's representative appointed for the duty who must comply with Rule 77 (a).

6. The Station Master or other person in charge must satisfy himself that these instructions are being strictly adhered to and he must specially report to the District Operating Superintendent every instance of failure of the Ground Frame Equipment.

Closure

Forcett Goods Station closed on 2 November 1964, and that part of the branch between Forcett Valley Junction and Forcett closed too. Thereafter, a major – if not the only – user of the Forcett Branch was British Railways' own Chief Civil Engineer, who obtained ballast from East Layton Quarry. However, in due course the supplies of stone suitable for use as ballast were exhausted. The Chief Civil Engineer therefore made alternative arrangements to obtain ballast from Broadwood, near Frosterley on the Wear Valley Branch.(50) These alternative arrangements having been put into effect, the entire remaining Forcett Branch from Forcett Junction to East Layton Quarries closed on Friday, 7 February or Monday, 2 May 1966; sources differ.

    Unlike the trackbed of the former Merrybent & Darlington Railway, much of which was used for a motorway, most of the route of the former Forcett Railway is just as the demolition men left it. Even Forcett engine shed still stands, in use as a workshop and garage. A major loss, however, is the viaduct over the Tees, demolished by J Stephenson & Company of Bishop Auckland in 1981.

The Merrybent & Darlington Railway

The underlying geology at Middleton Tyas (a parish in the North Riding of Yorkshire some nine miles south-west of Darlington) comprises carboniferous limestone. This stone has long been worked, both for building purposes and for sweetening acidic agricultural land. Within the limestone are found veins of copper and lead. Beginning in 1736, these veins were worked enthusiastically, so much so that much of the land surrounding the village of Middleton Tyas became riddled with shafts and workings underground, and covered in spoil heaps above ground. By the early 1780s, however, the veins were more or less worked out. Mining ceased and nature began to reclaim the shattered landscape.(51)

Nature had some eighty years in which to work its magic, but in April 1856 there were developments that threatened to undo all of its good work; some of the old mine workings were re-opened. Little work was done though, and nothing came of the endeavour. Instead, attention moved a few miles further north to the parish of Melsonby. In 1861, Christopher Lonsdale Bradley of Richmond leased from local landowners the right to mine minerals that might be found beneath their land, thereby becoming the owner of the Merrybent Estate. Bradley was an established mining entrepreneur, currently working the Hurst Mines near Marske. It was, however, his son Lonsdale Bradley who, with two partners, formed the Merrybent Mining Company to lease the mining rights from his father and to actually undertake the mining operations at Low Merrybent.

The enterprise was blessed with some success, and on 22 January 1863 a long column of some forty to fifty farm carts loaded with about 40 tons of copper ore set out from the newly-sunk mine to Piercebridge station, from where the ore would be conveyed by railway to Samuel Johnston & Company of Birkenhead for smelting. The farm carts were apparently provided free of charge; the prospects of jobs and business for local people evidently overcoming any scruples concerning the damage that mining operations might do to the landscape. At Piercebridge, Lonsdale Bradley hosted a cold collation in the Station Hotel and spoke enthusiastically of the future prospects for the Merrybent mine.

In total, 463 tons of copper ore were raised during 1863. The tonnage raised was less the following year, but this disappointment was assuaged by the raising of a significant tonnage of lead ore. In order to provide more money for investment in the mine, the Bradleys, father and son, and the other two partners in the Merrybent Mining Company (itself recently registered as a limited company) merged their interests to form, effective from 22 May 1865, the Merrybent and Middleton Tyas Mining and Smelting Company Limited. The Bradleys were shareholders, as were Lonsdale Bradley's two partners. Additional shareholders included Henry Currer Briggs, a director of Henry Briggs, Son & Company, a colliery company owning mines near Normanton in the West Riding of Yorkshire.

The next step in developing a successful mining enterprise was to organise rail transport – conveyance by farm cart was unsatisfactory in the long term. However, even if the additional investment in the mine greatly increased the tonnage of copper and lead ore to be conveyed, it was unlikely to be sufficient to cover the cost of constructing and operating a railway the six miles or so from the mine to the North Eastern Railway's Darlington & Barnard Castle Branch. Any railway would have to accept other traffic, and a potentially lucrative traffic was limestone from the quarries already being worked in the area.

As well as the traditional building and agricultural uses, this stone was in demand by the thriving iron works on Teesside. (The limestone was used as a flux in the blast furnaces.) Limestone for Teesside was currently being obtained from Weardale, about as far again from Teesside as was Melsonby parish. As well as limestone, the agricultural produce of the district would also provide traffic for the railway. Sadly for the mine owners, the directors of the North Eastern were not interested in constructing one. Undeterred, they decided to draw upon their own resources, and those of anybody else whom they could interest. One person who was very much interested was Robert Henry Allan, who owned land that could be quarried for limestone near the village of Barton.

Sufficient others also becoming involved, the promoters of the proposed railway formally set matters in train. Messrs Alexander Nimmo and Thomas F MacNay were appointed consulting engineers, and under their supervision plans and sections were prepared. An appeal in May 1866 by the directors of the nearby Forcett Railway Company to drop these plans, and instead to construct the railway as an extension of their own, thereby saving some £40,000, was rejected. It was felt that having an railway independent of another was worth the price. (Though, of course, the North Eastern Railway would be called upon to convey minerals onwards to their final destinations.) In due course, the Merrybent & Darlington Railway Company was incorporated by Act of Parliament on 11 June 1866.(52)

The troubles of the new railway company more or less began on that day. The directors appointed by the Act were: Robert Henry Allan (elected Chairman), Joseph Boyer, Christopher Lonsdale Bradley, Lonsdale Bradley, Henry Currer Briggs, John Harris and William Henry Wilson Todd. These men never really got a grip on the company from the day it was incorporated. The railway company offices were established in those of the mining company (*i.e.* the Merrybent and Middleton Tyas Mining and Smelting Company Limited) at 80 Bondgate, Darlington. The same man, Samuel Richardson (later sacked for incompetence) served as secretary for both companies. From the start, railway and mining companies were managed and operated as one concern. Indeed, one batch of stationary was headed 'The Merrybent Mining and Railway Company Limited', which had no legal existence.

Nimmo and MacNay had planned a railway branching off the North Eastern's Darlington & Barnard Castle Branch and running 6 miles 2 furlongs 13 yards to Street Field, which lay adjacent to Leeming Lane (forming part of the Great North Road). The main line of railway and short branch, 3 furlongs 43 yards long, would serve the limestone quarries Allan and Boyer intended to open on their lands to the west and south-west of Barton, and, on the other side of Leeming Lane, mines and quarries on the Merrybent Estate and a freestone quarry on Gatherley Moor. A tramway would provide the connection to the latter; constructed across land owned by the parties concerned, it would not need parliamentary sanction. There was also a proposal to connect with the Forcett Railway, to what end is not clear.

The registered capital of the railway company was £60,000 in the form of 6000 £10 shares. The directors of the company were each required to buy 50 shares; one fifth of the value of each share was to be paid at once. However, no shares were ever actually allocated, and the whole of the capital remained in trust with the mining company. The railway company was also allowed to raise £20,000 in loans, and much of the money for the construction of the railway was raised in this way. (Where the money came from, and where it went, was not easy to determine, as the company's books were chaotically kept.) With what money was to hand, the appointed contractors, Messrs Lovel and Jones, set to work.

Meanwhile, within a few months of the granting of the Act, George Leeman (deputy chairman of the North Eastern and a financial backer of the Merrybent & Darlington) proposed a formal association between the mining company and the railway company. Legal advice was sought, and the upshot was that the mining company was reconstituted as the New Merrybent and Middleton Tyas Mining and Smelting Company Limited. Which was all very well, but did not assist with the task of winning copper and lead from the ground. There was no copper ore raised in 1866, though 205 tons of lead ore was raised. The poor financial returns precipitated a financial crisis. Christopher

Henry King Spark (1825 - 1899) was a major driving force and investor in the Merrybent mining and railway ventures, eventually controlling both. Their subsequent liquidation resulted in Spark being made bankrupt in 1876. A colourful character and a practised orator with a persuasive tongue, he was described by his enemies as a 'vainglorious braggart'. At one time he was the proprietor of 'The Darlington & Stockton Times' and he made three unsuccessful attempts to represent Darlington in Parliament. He would retire in some disgrace to Penrith and later to Barnard Castle where he would die a rather lonely bachelor. (Centre for Local Studies at Darlington Library)

Lonsdale Bradley, an experienced mining entrepreneur, was ousted, and in 1868 Henry King Spark of Darlington and a significant financial backer of the Merrybent & Darlington, gained effective control. Henceforth, the requirements of the railway company would take precedence over those of the mining company.

Construction of the railway proceeded, though at a leisurely pace; according to the Act, the railway was supposed to be completed within three years of its being passed. Nor was the construction work done particularly well. When William Bewick Quelch was appointed by the railway company as resident engineer in February 1869, he discovered that what track had been laid was on cheap untreated sleepers, which were already rotting. Quelch was instructed to see that the contractors used good quality Swedish or Norwegian timber, and to supervise the creosoting of the sleepers cut from it. He was also required to consult with Nimmo and MacNay about the possibility of reducing the cost of the large bridge being built over the River Tees by Messrs Hopkins, Gilkes & Company Limited of Middlesbrough. Bizarrely, Nimmo and MacNay acknowledged Quelch's authority in a letter they wrote to him but refused to do so in a letter to the contractors Lovel and Jones. The services of the consulting engineers were therefore dispensed with, and the contractors told firmly to abide by Quelch's instructions.

Meanwhile, in anticipation of the completion of the railway, Robert Allan employed an agent to deal with the sale of his limestone. However, the advice that the new agent gave was not encouraging. He told Allan that it was well known that Pease & Partners sold their ironstone only to those who also contracted to buy their limestone. The Forcett Railway, under the chairmanship of Carl Bolckow, had been handling traffic from February 1867. The bulk of this traffic was limestone, bound for Bolckow, Vaughan & Company Limited's ironworks on Teesside. Given these facts, the opportunities for selling limestone from the quarries around Barton were bound to be limited.

Nevertheless, construction of the railway was well advanced, and the secretary inserted a notice in the 1 January 1870 issue of *The Darlington & Stockton Times*.

As things transpired, the railway was not ready for opening on 1 January 1870. By March though, the secretary felt confident enough to insert a notice in the 26 March issue of *The Darlington & Stockton Times* to the effect that the railway would be opened for traffic on 2 May. Probably because of the delayed Board of Trade inspection on the newly-doubled section of the Darlington & Barnard Castle Branch (see page 52 and below), it was not until 1 June 1870 that a train chartered from the North Eastern departed Darlington at about 11 o'clock with a party of some 200 ladies and gentlemen bound for the Merrybent & Darlington's opening ceremony. Approaching Merrybent Junction, the party observed with satisfaction the new rails on the formerly single-track Darlington & Barnard Castle, now doubled as far as Piercebridge in anticipation of heavy traffic off the Merrybent & Darlington (and, of course, off the Forcett Railway, which made a junction with the North Eastern a few miles to the west of Piercebridge). Beyond the junction, the train stopped so that the North Eastern's locomotive could be detached, and the Merrybent & Darlington's attached.

A view of Merrybent Junction looking west towards Barnard Castle, 20 January 1953. The Merrybent Branch bears away to the left. The overbridge in the distance carries a farm track over the Darlington & Barnard Castle Branch. The first signal box at Merrybent Junction was opened in June 1870 at the same time as the Merrybent & Darlington opened to traffic. The box contained a McKenzie, Clunes & Holland 6" pitch, 14-lever frame, which had been built in 1869. Thirteen of these levers were working. The base of this first signal box is just beyond the tall signal box seen here, cut down and in use by platelayers. The signal box so prominent in the photograph was commissioned in 1907; a new McKenzie & Holland, 5" pitch No 16 pattern 25-lever frame was provided. In the mid 1920s, 16 levers were working and nine were spare.

From late October 1894, Merrybent Junction was one of the locations used to test Assistant Locomotive Superintendent Vincent Raven's Fog Signal Apparatus. Fitted in a locomotive cab and triggered by track-mounted levers connected to the relevant distant signal, this warned an engine driver if he passed that signal when it was 'on'. Passing a signal without seeing it was all too easily done when it was shrouded by fog. Apart from the test locations, the apparatus was only ever installed on the main line north of York. (JW Armstrong / Armstrong Railway Photographic Trust)

The Merrybent & Darlington Railway's 'Merrybent', an outside cylinder saddle tank. As originally built, the locomotive did not have a cab, merely a spectacle plate. The cab seen here was fitted at the NER's Darlington Works, possibly after the railway company's acquisition of the M&DR. Other minor changes were made to the locomotive, such as the fitting of the NER-pattern chimney. (NERA Collection GMP10_0031)

Merrybent, an 0-6-0ST newly-built by Messrs Hopper, Radcliffe & Company, took the train forward. It was stopped briefly on the bridge over the Tees so that interested members of the party could make an inspection. At the terminus of the line, Barton station, the train stopped again, the band played, and the party made its way on foot to the mine where an inspection of selected samples of ore took place. Then it was back to Barton, where luncheon was provided in a large marquee. The chairman of the railway company, Henry King Spark, who now controlled both the mining and the railway companies, gave a very optimistic speech after lunch, which was, more or less, well received. However, the financial backers of the railway company were disappointed that the promised short branch had not yet been constructed, and members of the public were disappointed that the promised passenger service did not seem likely to materialise. (Robert Allan was no longer chairman of the railway company; he had found the situation of his being both a director and a major creditor of the company distinctly uncomfortable.)(53)

Disappointment concerning the lack of progress on constructing the branch soon turned to anguish as both the railway and the mining companies struggled with discouraging cash flows. Little ore was coming out of the mine, and relatively little limestone was being quarried as the market for limestone flux was already being well served from elsewhere. In September 1870 Robert Allan precipitated a financial crisis when he sought re-payment of a loan to the railway company. There followed an extended period of boardroom turmoil, as anxious directors and their supporters mounted coup after coup. In 1874, the North Eastern seized the railway in lieu of debt; the matter was soon resolved, in the short term at least.

When directors and their supporters were not plotting against each other, some useful work was done. While Henry Currer Briggs was serving as chairman of the railway company, he obtained a two-year extension under the Railways (Extension of Time) Act, 1869, giving at least the opportunity of constructing the missing branch. However, both the mining and the railway companies continued to struggle financially. The mining company was liquidated, its failure leading to the bankruptcy of Henry King Spark. The fixed assets of the company were sold at auction on 29 April 1878 to Robert Allan. The movable assets – huts, tools, wagons, *etc.* – were sold on 25 June. All these latter were dispersed, and hereafter Allan would work the Merrybent Estate solely for its limestone. (Mining for copper and lead would be undertaken, on and off, in a modest way by other parties over the years that followed, but to no significant effect.)

The Merrybent & Darlington Railway Company was dissolved by Act of Parliament on 17 June 1878.(54) It was thereby acquired by the Darlington District Joint Stock Banking Company, the major creditor. In that year the railway was examined by an NER Permanent Way Inspector, who reported that rotten sleepers rendered the track unsafe for any locomotive larger than a small tank locomotive, and that none of the company's locomotives or rolling stock should be allowed on to the line. If no NER wagons were allowed on the line, then no traffic could run. The railway would thus appear to have lain derelict for some time, though it is not clear for how long. A Preliminary Announcement concerning the sale by public auction of the Merrybent & Darlington Railway was published in *The Darlington & Stockton Times* on 12 January 1884; the railway was described as a 'going concern'. This implies that trains were running, an implication confirmed by the NER's traffic records which show that in 1885 Barton Goods Station forwarded 9949 tons of goods and received 5418 tons. (The goods forwarded tonnage was unusually high for the period; tonnage would fall to 443 in 1888, thereafter climbing again. No contemporary figures are available for the tonnage of limestone forwarded.)

However, there is no mention of the railway in the index of single lines in the NER's *Appendix A to the Working Time Table* effective from 1 January 1898, so at this time no North Eastern locomotives were working traffic over the former Merrybent & Darlington.

Whether the public auction of the railway ever took place is not known. Perhaps not, as the North Eastern acquired the railway in 1890, though an appropriate Act of Parliament was not obtained until 30 July 1900.(55)

A Description of the NER's Merrybent Branch

The Merrybent Branch (also described in North Eastern documents as the Barton Branch) began at Merrybent Junction, 1 mile 66 chains from the zero point of the North Eastern's Darlington & Barnard Castle Branch at Hopetown Junction. The Siding Diagram reproduced here shows the arrangement in 1914. The headshunt (No 3 on the drawing) was 140 yards long, of which 91 yards were available for standage. The exchange siding (No 1) was 339 yards long, of which 165 yards were available for standage. For much of the existence of the line, wagons to and from Barton and the mines and quarries beyond were exchanged at the junction. It was to bring wagons to the junction, and to take them back up the Merrybent & Darlington Railway, that the locomotive *Merrybent* was obtained.

From the exchange siding, the single-track railway ran approximately south-south-west towards the River Tees. Just over one and a quarter miles from Merrybent Junction were situated Coniscliffe Depot and Siding. There were four coal cells at the depot, and the siding (No 1 on the drawing) was 260 yards long, of which 150 yards were available for standage. In 1898, the depot was noted as generating coal traffic both for Darlington Corporation's and Stockton & Middlesbrough Corporations' separate water works at Low Coniscliffe.(56) *Instructions to Agents*, published in 1918, showed some changes had occurred in the years since 1898. Coniscliffe Depot now handled the traffic of Darlington Corporation and the Tees Valley Water Board. It is most likely that this traffic was coal, brought in to feed the steam engines powering the pumps used to supply Darlington and Teesside with drinking water. Coniscliffe Siding was for full wagon loads only, as Smalls were to be sent to Darlington (Bank Top).

Approaching the River Tees, the branch curved to the south-east to cross the river at right angles. The bridge, No 11 on the branch, was erected by Hopkins, Gilkes & Company Limited, better known perhaps as the constructors of the ill-fated Tay Bridge. The Tees Bridge would prove to be more long lasting, though it was lightly constructed. It was built under the supervision of Lieutenant-Colonel W Hawdon, the two pairs of cast iron piers being sunk some 30 feet through the river bottom to bedrock. The three 74' 8" spans comprised wrought-iron lattice girders between brick-arched masonry abutments; the deck was timber.

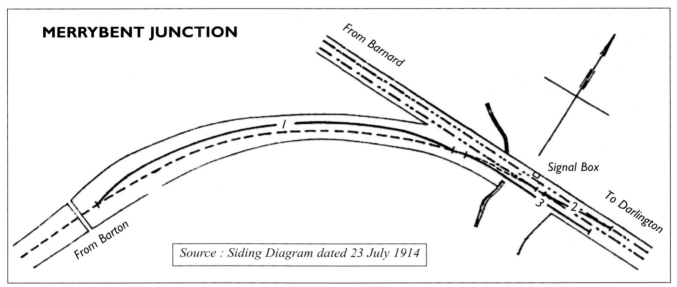

MERRYBENT JUNCTION

Source : Siding Diagram dated 23 July 1914

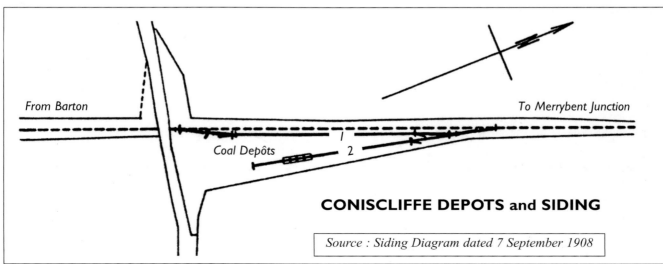

From Barton

To Merrybent Junction

Coal Depôts

CONISCLIFFE DEPOTS and SIDING

Source : Siding Diagram dated 7 September 1908

A Trip on the "Merrybent"

The Northern Despatch, 23 February 1948

I learn from Councillor W.B. Eggleston of Barton that the old Merrybent and Darlington Railway, about which we wrote last week, did in fact occasionally carry passengers. Councillor Eggleston should know, for he himself travelled on the line taking a ride on the locomotive "Merrybent". He writes,

"Apart from the fact that in May 1896 the late Mr. George Hildreth (the Barton Schoolmaster) and I boarded the locomotion 'Merrybent' when returning from measuring the 'away-going' crops of the late Herbert Johnson of High House, Cleasby, my wife tells me that she was a fare paying passenger on a 'special train' which ran from Barton to Coniscliffe Siding on the occasion of the Royal Show held at Hummersknott Park in June 1895.

The 'carriages' were open trucks fitted with wooden seats. The locomotive driver would be the late Mr. John Howe, and the fireman his brother, the late Mr. George Howe. The guard would probably be Mr. Joseph P. Howe who was Stationmaster at Barton for many years though whether he carried a flag and whistle is not remembered.

Writing of the Merrybent Railway has reminded me that in the Summer of 1891 I spent a day as a Clerk at the age of eight – shades of Dickens – at Barton Station. My brother was the Clerk at Barton Station and he wanted a day off with the Wesleyan School scholars but the Stationmaster, Mr. Jos. Howe, insisted that I deputize, which I did."

Darlington shed's Class J25 No 5648 is seen here passing the exchange siding at Merrybent Junction (No 1 on the Siding Diagram) in the late 1940s. Before the NER took over the operation of the Merrybent & Darlington Railway, its locomotives ventured no further than this point. No 5648 would itself not venture much further as members of the class were deemed too heavy for the Tees Bridge. (JW Armstrong / Armstrong Railway Photographic Trust)

This photograph of Coniscliffe Depots and Siding was taken on 16 November 1952 when the railway was being lifted. The four coal cells initially served the steam engines at the water works pumping stations a short cart ride eastwards. The glasshouses comprising Merrybent Nurseries on either side of the line were constructed by the Co-operative Wholesale Society in the 1930s, and the coal cells may well have served them too. (Note the chimneys indicating that at least some of them were heated.) (JW Armstrong / Armstrong Railway Photographic Trust)

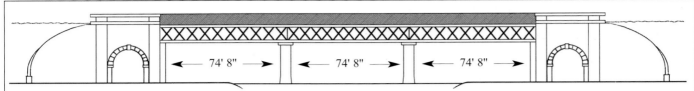

BRICK ARCH. STONE FACE & ABUTS.   BRICK ARCH. STONE FACE & ABUTS.

W. I. LATTICE GIRDERS, CROSS TIMBERS & TIMBER DECK.

Bridge No 11 : *Tees Bridge*, Low Coniscliffe

Source for sketch : Engineer's Line Diagram

Alexander Nimmo and Thomas F MacNay were engaged as consulting engineers for the construction of the M&DR. Initially the Tees Bridge at Low Coniscliffe was built according to their design by Hopkins, Gilkes & Company Limited. However, it would appear that to save money the design was modified during the course of the build; it may have been for this reason that the deck was supported by cross timbers rather than by wrought-iron girders. The relatively weak deck would limit the size of locomotive that was permitted to cross it. For many years only 0-6-0 tank locomotives were permitted; after the Second World War the LNER authorised passage by 0-6-0 tender locomotives of Class J24. (W Rogerson / Ken Hoole Study Centre Collection)

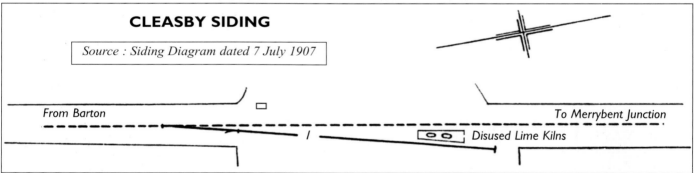

CLEASBY SIDING

Source : Siding Diagram dated 7 July 1907

From Barton   To Merrybent Junction

Disused Lime Kilns

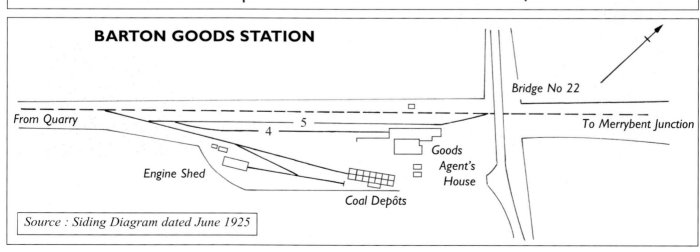

BARTON GOODS STATION

Bridge No 22

From Quarry   To Merrybent Junction

Engine Shed

Goods Agent's House

Coal Depôts

Source : Siding Diagram dated June 1925

On the far side of the river, the railway was routed between Howden Hill and Cleasby. The railway curved to the right here, henceforth running in an approximate south-south-westerly direction towards Barton. Cleasby Siding, not quite 3 miles from Merrybent Junction, was in 1898 recorded as serving the Barton Limestone Company Limited. The Siding Diagram reproduced here shows that by 1907 the lime kilns were disused, and in 1918 the siding is noted as being for use by the general public.

A late addition to the branch was Newton Morrell Siding, not quite four and a half miles from Merrybent Junction. This siding was not recorded in 1898 as the agreement between Murrough John Wilson, Samuel Hugh Rowlandson and the North Eastern was not signed until 22 December 1903. The siding was used for agricultural purposes; annual rent was £7 10s.

By 1918 the siding was noted as serving GW and AE Corner and MJ Wilson's tenants. On the North Eastern's Line Diagram, thought to have been drawn in the 1920s, the siding is simply marked 'Rowlandsons'.

The railway passed between Brettanby Manor and Barton. Just over five miles from Merrybent Junction was Barton Goods Station, situated to the north-west of the village. There was a house here for the Goods Agent, plus sidings, loading docks, coal depots and an engine shed and water tank. Siding No 5 on the drawing was 229 yards long, of which 150 yards were available for standage; on a Siding Diagram of 1933, this siding is labelled 'Exchange Sidings'. Siding No 4 was 154 yards long, of which 109 yards were available for standage; there was a loading gauge on this siding, suspended above the rails beyond the end of the loading dock.

This view looks southwards along Cleasby Cutting. The cutting was the only major earthwork on the M&DR. It also provided the line's stiffest gradient at 1 in 61. The cutting appears to be fenced by quickset hedges, neatly trimmed. (W Rogerson / Ken Hoole Study Centre Collection)

Barton Goods Station viewed from Bridge No 22 carrying the Barton - Manfield Road. Designed by an architect called Swan at an estimated cost of £527 17s 9d, it is of ridiculously generous proportions for a railway terminus that was never likely to generate large volumes of traffic for a company that was perennially struggling for funds. Having said that, on the occasion of the photograph the station yard is busy... Principal traffic forwarded comprised roadstone (3330 tons in 1907), sand, barley, hay and clover, potatoes, wheat, timber, building stone, loam and livestock.

In addition to this traffic, here we see that wagons loaded with limestone have been brought from Barton Quarry, which is away through the bridge to the right; a quarry locomotive is bringing additional wagons. There is a second locomotive in the small goods yard, which is packed with wagons and an NER Diagram V1 brake van; the guard has his stove lit, as may be discerned from the smoke coming from the chimney.

Despite the platform provided at Barton, there would never be a regular passenger service. (WB Eggleston / John Alsop Collection A380)

Another two views of Barton Goods Station. In the upper photograph, the van was built between 1903 and 1905 to Diagram G2; it is in rather faded LNER early livery (as applied between 1923 and 1937). In the lower photograph, note the earthen ramp adjacent to siding No 4, apparently built to allow road-going vehicles to tip their contents into railway wagons. (Both photographs, NERA KL Taylor Collection)

Barton Goods Station had a busy year in 1903 when Goods Forwarded totalled 31,443 tons and Goods Received 4841 tons. In addition, 6717 tons of 'Coal, Coke, Lime and Limestone' were received, a large proportion of which was coal which passed over the cells seen here (derelict) on 22 April 1963. (This tonnage did not include limestone despatched from the quarries: 147,120 tons in 1908, for example.) Total receipts in 1903 were £2747, included in which was £13 for 'Parcels, Horses, Carriages, Dogs &c.' Station expenses came to £189.(RV Webster)

Above : The former engine shed and its associated water tank on 22 April 1963. The ruinous structure on the far right appears to have been built as a base for the original water tank. On some unknown date, that tank was replaced by the one seen to its left, assembled from typical NER cast iron plates. This tank may have been built new at Barton, or the plates may have been salvaged from a tank replaced elsewhere. There is a number near the bottom of the left-hand front plate – D4 perhaps, or D41? – indicating that maintenance of the tank was the responsibility of Darlington shed. In the centre of the plate is the number D20, the number of the water column. (RV Webster)

'Barton' is the Henry Hughes & Company 0-4-0ST initially obtained to work NER wagons between Barton Goods Station and Barton Quarry. Three additional locomotives would be obtained to work both Barton and Merrybent Quarries, and below is Barton Limestone Company Limited's No 3 'Melsonby'. The livery is typical of locomotives built by Manning, Wardle at this time. The locomotives, and 'Merrybent', are maintained, fuelled and watered at Barton engine shed.

NER traffic records show the following tonnages of limestone despatched from the quarries: 1906, 114,614 tons; 1907, 140,269 tons; 1908, 147,120 tons. (Photographs courtesy John and Edith Davison, per Chris Lloyd of The Northern Echo)

Barton Quarry Relief Siding, 149 yards long (95 yards standage), was situated just less than 5¾ miles from the junction. The end of the branch, and the end point of North Eastern maintenance, was precisely 5 miles 67.97 chains from the junction. Sidings fanned out from the final few yards of the branch to the various working faces of Barton Quarry, operated by the Barton Limestone Company Limited. At a later date, a new quarry, Merrybent Quarry, would be opened and served by sidings connected to the railway.

The Working of Traffic on the Merrybent Branch
In the Merrybent & Darlington's Act of Parliament incorporating the company were specific provisions allowing it to enter into agreements with the North Eastern for such as maintenance, the joint use of stations and sidings, the supply of rolling stock and staff, and the working and interchange of traffic. These provisions were made use of, and suitable arrangements made.

When the Merrybent & Darlington formally opened, on 1 June 1870, the track reached only as far as Barton station. However, a siding was subsequently laid to the quarry, and an 0-4-0ST – named *Barton* – was bought circa 1872 from Henry Hughes & Company in order to work North Eastern wagons between the quarry and Barton Goods Station. From the station, loaded wagons were conveyed by *Merrybent* to the exchange siding at Merrybent Junction. It is not clear when this traffic actually started. The North Eastern's Northern Division *Working Time Table* effective from 1 September 1870 noted the existence of Merrybent Junction, but had no trains stopping there.

As was standard practice with railway company Acts of Parliament, the maximum permissible tolls for the diverse classes of goods were stipulated in the Merrybent & Darlington's Act. There were within the Act too maximum tolls for passenger traffic, and details as to how much luggage the various classes of passenger were permitted to carry free of charge. It would seem that there was a definite intention to operate a passenger service on the railway. During a court hearing in connection with the assessment of damage to agricultural land sustained by its construction, the railway company's legal representative, EJ Meynell, stated that Barton station 'is being built so that it will accommodate passenger traffic'.(57) From study of records in British Railways' archives, the late Ken Hoole thought that, for a time at least, passenger trains had indeed run from the station.(58) However, these records have not been found by the present authors. If passenger trains did operate on the Merrybent & Darlington, they were not, apparently, running when the North Eastern issued its *Working Time Table* effective from 1 September 1870. Passenger traffic, it ever there was any, was short lived. Attempts by local people early in the Twentieth Century to persuade the North Eastern to operate passenger trains between Barton and Darlington fell on deaf ears.

The next working timetable examined for the purposes of this book was current from 1 October 1897 to 30 April 1898 (*i.e.* after the purchase of the

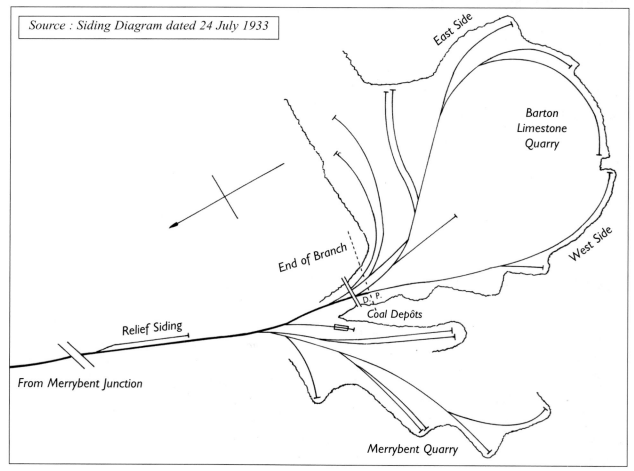

Source : Siding Diagram dated 24 July 1933

East Side

Barton Limestone Quarry

West Side

End of Branch

D. P.

Coal Depôts

Relief Siding

From Merrybent Junction

Merrybent Quarry

Merrybent & Darlington by the North Eastern). It showed that Train No 15, the 7:25 am Goods from North Road to Bowes, stopped as required at Merrybent Junction. It seems likely that this pick-up goods dropped empty wagons at the exchange siding on its way out to Bowes, and picked up wagons loaded with stone and with copper and lead ore on its return to North Road (as Train No 27, the 12:50 pm Goods from Bowes to North Road).

Barton Goods Station was arranged to handle conventional goods traffic, and it seems likely also that the pick-up goods conveyed this in addition to the traffic in stone and ore. From what can be gathered, by

1898 *Merrybent* had been sold, and the haulage of wagons between Barton Goods Station and Merrybent Junction was being undertaken by a North Eastern locomotive working from Darlington shed. The North Eastern worked the single-line Merrybent Branch by train staff, as a single section. The North Eastern's 1922 *Appendix to the General Rules and Regulations…* describes the train staff simply as a 'Round brass staff'. It was kept by the signalman at Merrybent Junction, and issued to a driver as he drove his train on to the branch. The LNER's *Sectional Appendix* dated 1 November 1947 states that the points at Coniscliffe and Cleasby Sidings were secured by chains and

These two views are of Barton Quarry circa 1905. In the upper photograph, most of the wagons in the rake in the foreground are NER Central Division mineral wagons. The two wagons at the far end of the rake may be quarry company internal user wagons as one has dumb buffers and the other is not as high as the others. Note the timber trestles spanning the quarry; these carry narrow gauge field railway track for use in removing the quarry overburden.

The lower photograph gives a clearer view of how the quarry encroaches upon the surrounding farmland. The overburden is being removed by means of a hand-propelled skip and a light field railway. The two wagons pushed up to the quarry face are NER mineral wagons. The tracks upon which the wagons run are roughly laid, comprising flat-bottomed rails spiked to wooden sleepers. (Both photographs courtesy John and Edith Davison, per Chris Lloyd of The Northern Echo)

padlocks; the keys to the padlocks were attached to the train staff.

Four locomotives are recorded as operated by Barton Limestone Company Limited, all being 0-4-0ST locomotives: *Barton*, as previously described; No 3 *Melsonby*, built by Manning, Wardle in 1906; No 2 *Barton*, built by Manning, Wardle in 1908; No 1 *Merrybent*, built by R&W Hawthorn, Leslie in 1914.(59) The latter was sold or hired to Pease & Partners Limited for use at that company's Rogerley Quarry, Frosterley, as early as 1915.(60)

As to the North Eastern's locomotives, the April 1917 issue of *Loads of Engines Working Freight Trains* stipulated that only 0-6-0T locomotives of Classes 290 and E were permitted to work on the Barton Branch. (The use of 0-6-0T locomotives of Class E1 was sanctioned subsequently.) Maximum load of a Class C mineral or concentrated goods train from Barton Quarry to Merrybent Junction was 385 tons for a locomotive of Class E, 495 tons for a Class 290. (After the Second World War, the LNER would introduce a Route Availability scheme for its locomotives. The branch would be classified as RA2, allowing 0-6-0 locomotives of Class J24 to traverse it also.)

Loads of Engines Working Freight Trains also stipulated a train length of 40 goods or mineral wagons between Merrybent Junction and Coniscliffe, but no more than 28 wagons between Coniscliffe and Barton. The reduced train length between the latter two places was because a locomotive could run round no more than 28 wagons at Barton.

The volume of stone traffic off the Merrybent Branch was not sustained, and the LNER (North Eastern Area) working timetable in effect from 8 April to 7 July 1929 showed only one mineral train per day to Barton: Train No 24, the 8:10 am Class C Mineral from Darlington to Barton, which shunted en route at Albert Hill between 8:20 and 9 am. The pick-up goods was no longer booked to stop at Merrybent Junction at all; perhaps the modest goods traffic of the branch was conveyed by Train No 24.

By the time that the working timetable in effect from 4 July to 25 September 1938 was issued, stone traffic had declined to such an extent that the traffic to and from both Barton and Forcett Quarry were being dealt with by the same train; Train No 38, the 9:15 am Class C Goods from North Road West Sidings to Barton and Forcett Quarry. The working timetable in effect from 25 September 1939 to 28 April 1940 showed a similar Class C Goods, departing from North Road West Sidings at 8:45 am.

Rail traffic from the quarry ceased in 1946. On 16 August, the managing director of the Barton Limestone Company, William Benjamin Eggleston, ticketed out the last wagon of limestone; it was the last of a large order destined for Dorman, Long & Company's Britannia Steelworks in Middlesbrough. The Barton Limestone Company went into voluntary liquidation about this time, and in November the quarries, surrounding farm land and cottages were acquired by Eggleston.(61) Henceforth, he would send out limestone by road, not rail. The sidings to the quarries were lifted and the quarry company locomotives disposed of.

Coal, agricultural and other traffic continued to be worked over the branch; in January 1950, a letter from the District Goods Manager (DGM) in connection with his recommendation that the branch be closed owing to financial losses stated that Barton Goods Station was handling 36 wagons a month.(62) The DGM also said that there were alternative goods facilities at Forcett, Croft and Piercebridge.

The DGM's recommendation to the Railway Executive was accepted, and the Merrybent & Darlington Branch closed formally to goods traffic on Monday, 3 July 1950 (the last revenue-earning train had run on Saturday, 1 July). Work started in 1952 to lift the redundant track and to demolish the bridges; *The Darlington & Stockton Times* reported on 1 November 1952 that the iron from the bridge was required for the nation's re-armament programme.

Much of the trackbed of the branch was subsequently utilised for the $10^1/_2$ miles long A1(M) Darlington By-Pass and is now buried beneath the motorway. The first sod of the by-pass was cut by the Minister of Transport, Ernest Marples, on 6 May 1963. During the work that followed, the station building at Barton was demolished and a new quarry opened to provide fill for embankments and sub-base for the road. The trackbed of the single-track railway had to be widened to 105 feet in order to accommodate the by-pass.(63) The completed by-pass was opened by Tom Fraser, successor to Marples, on Friday, 14 May 1965.

The Tees Bridge during demolition in 1952. In the course of the work, the wooden deck of the bridge was accidentally set on fire. The arrival of the viaduct had been regretted by the boatman who had ferried folk across the river, but suddenly found his customers preferred to trespass over the bridge than pay the fare; its departure was regretted by anglers who found it a very useful short cut in their bid to gain a promising pitch on the 'other side'. (JW Armstrong / Armstrong Railway Photographic Trust)

Merrybent

As noted in the chapter describing the Merrybent & Darlington Railway, in 1870 Messrs Hopper, Radcliffe & Company's Britannia Iron Works, Fencehouses, County Durham built *Merrybent*. The locomotive is shown in the drawing below in its as-built condition.

The locomotive was an outside cylinder saddle tank. Cylinder dimensions were 13" x 20"; wheels were 3' 7½" diameter, located in a wheelbase of 11' 2" equally divided. The boiler was 3' 6" in diameter, 9' long and contained 92 brass tubes each of 1¾" outside diameter; working pressure was 120 pounds per square inch. Boiler feed water was supplied from the 600 gallon tank via a Giffard injector and pump. The firebox was 3' 10" long. Bunker capacity was about 1¼ tons of coal. In working order, the locomotive weighed 24 tons 4 cwt. Axle weights were: leading, 9 tons 12 cwt; driving, 7 tons 6 cwt; trailing, 7 tons 6 cwt.

Perhaps the most interesting thing about the locomotive though is why Hopper, Radcliffe & Company actually built it. The company was a substantial concern, manufacturing, among other things, locomotive and tender axles, wagon axles and wheels and even complete coal wagons. In 1869 it had even built a locomotive : an 0-4-0ST named *Britannia*. However, although a steam locomotive engine was essentially a simple piece of machinery, to design one from scratch was still a time-consuming business. And once the design had been finalised, patterns would be required to make the diverse components. Locomotive-building specialists such as Kitson & Company spread the cost of design and pattern-making over a large number of more or less identical locomotives. One wonders how Hopper, Radcliffe could hope to compete against these specialist builders. Perhaps capacity in the works was otherwise spare, and locomotive building in a modest way was thought to be a productive way of using it.

George Hopper's son and a partner in the business, John Ingledew Hopper, was a mining engineer, and perhaps this interest provided the link between Hopper, Radcliffe and the promoters of the Merrybent & Darlington Railway (who, of course, were very much involved with the mining of copper and lead at Low Merrybent). Anyway, an order was placed by the promoters for an 0-6-0 saddle tank for the main hauls from Barton to the exchange siding at Merrybent Junction.

It is not known how much of the locomotive was actually made in the Britannia Iron Works. Perhaps major components such as the boiler, firebox and cylinder block were bought in from outside suppliers, and the rest of the locomotive was built around these. What is known is that the overall design was drawn up by Thomas Hudson, who also supervised its erection. One obvious feature of the locomotive that resulted is the square-shaped water tank. No doubt this square shape was selected as it minimised the number of plates that had to be rolled to match the curve of the boiler. Another clue to the origins of the locomotive in the works of a non-specialist builder was the simple, if not downright crude, smokebox door arrangement. The price charged to the M&DR for the locomotive was £1,120 less 5% discount; it would be interesting to know how much it had actually cost to build.

The service history of *Merrybent* is not known, but it presumably gave some satisfaction at least, as it served the M&DR throughout its entire existence. Hopper, Radcliffe went on to build – or so it is thought – four more locomotives, but the business failed in 1874 due, in part at least, to a depression in trade. One can only speculate as to the part, if there was one, that locomotive building played in the company's demise. It may be significant, however, that when a locomotive was required to work wagons between Barton station and the quarry, one was obtained not from Hopper,

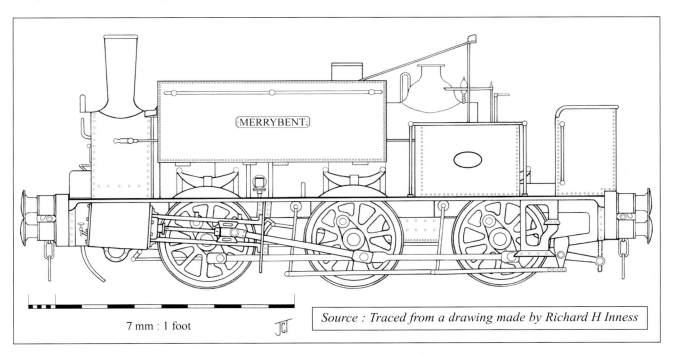

7 mm : 1 foot

JGI

Source : Traced from a drawing made by Richard H Inness

Radcliffe, but from Henry Hughes & Company (the 0-4-0ST subsequently named *Barton*).

Major repairs to *Merrybent* were carried out at Darlington works by the NER. The second drawing and the photographs show minor changes that took place during these repairs. The most significant change, at least as far as the enginemen were concerned, was that a cab was fitted in place of the original spectacle plate. An NER-pattern chimney was fitted, and a second sandbox on the left-hand side in front of the cab sheeting. The sand from this box was useful in both forward and rearwards motion, unlike that from the original box, which was useful only when the locomotive was moving forwards. Also on the left-hand side, a tool box was fitted next to the smokebox. (This may well have been fitted by those in charge of day to day maintenance, rather than by the NER.) To improve brake performance, the original wood brake blocks were replaced with ones of cast iron. Other changes included the replacement of the original secondary buffers with dumb buffers, and the fitting of a screw-down lid to the water tank. Perhaps the most interesting change made was the application of TW Worsdell's standard Saxony green and claret livery, first seen in March 1886 on the newly-built locomotives of Class A. The livery was expensive to apply, both in terms of paint and painters' time, and one assumes that those responsible at North Road supposed that the NER would take *Merrybent* into stock (though the locomotive was not lettered 'N.E.R.'). This did not happen, and circa 1890 *Merrybent* was sold to Robert Fraser of Hebburn. Circa 1903, Fraser sold the locomotive to the contractor JW Lant who was engaged upon the task of constructing the NER's Ponteland Branch. That task having been completed, it was sold again to a North Shields scrapman and broken up in 1905.

A front view of 'Merrybent', possibly taken in 1890 after the acquisition of the Merrybent & Darlington Railway by the NER. The livery applied is NER Locomotive Superintendent Thomas William Worsdell's Saxony green and claret livery, fully lined out in black bordered white and vermilion. This standard NER livery does not seem to be newly applied, as the paint on the dumb buffers appears to be bruised. (NERA Collection GMP10_0032)

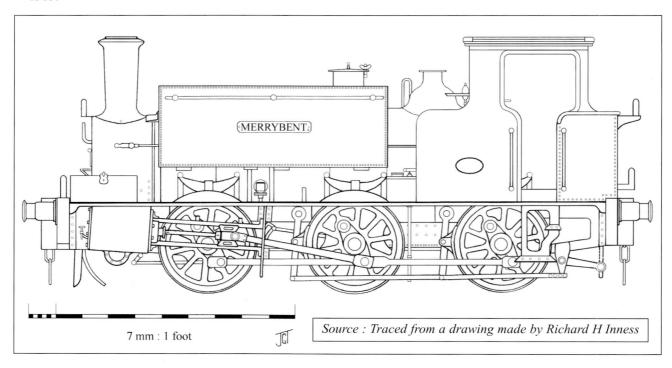

MERRYBENT.

7 mm : 1 foot

Source : Traced from a drawing made by Richard H Inness

Endnotes

Fighting Cocks Branch

(1) 1 & 2 Geo IV, Cap xliv *An Act for making and maintaining a Railway or Tramroad from the River Tees at Stockton to Witton Park Colliery with several Branches therefrom, all in the County of Durham.*

(2) 4 Geo IV, Cap xxxiii *An Act to enable the Stockton and Darlington Railway Company to vary and alter the Line of their Railway, and also the Line or Lines of some of the Branches therefrom, and to make an additional Branch therefrom, and for altering and enlarging the Powers of the Act passed for making and maintaining the said Railway.*

(3) See such as the NER's *Appendix B to the General Rules and Regulations…*, from 1 January 1898 and until further notice.

(4) Signal box opening times from *Appendix B to the General Rules and Regulations…*, from 1 January 1898 and until further notice.

(5) The only known use of Fighting Cocks by passengers after closure in 1887 occurred during the S&DR Centenary celebrations in 1925. A train of wagons was decorated with diverse tableaux to illustrate the 'Evolution of the Wheel'. After rolling past the crowds at Stockton, the train stopped at Fighting Cocks to allow the actors to get off the open wagons and into a train of *Flying Scotsman* carriages for the return run. So for a brief period, the platform was filled with Stone Age men, ancient Egyptians *etc*. Sadly, no photograph of the scene has yet been discovered… On the same day, the GWR's *Windsor Castle*, hauling the Royal Train, arrived at Fighting Cocks for a loco change. *Viscount Churchill* took over the Royal Train for the onward journey south via Eaglescliffe, while *Windsor Castle* coupled to a set of GWR articulated carriages and took them back to Faverdale for public display.

(6) TNA MT 6/709/1. *Inspection Report on Arrangements for the Royal Show*, 1895.

(7) See also TNA RAIL 667/1195. S&D Crossing, Correspondence between the S&DR and the York, Newcastle & Berwick Railway (formed in 1847 following the amalgamation of the companies serving those places).

(8) *The Northern Echo*, 6 September 1872, *Life on the Line : In a Signal Cabin*. No 27 in the series *Local Industrial Sketches*.

(9) Joint Ken Hoole Study Centre / NERA JF Mallon Collection JFM5545. Accident report.

(10) The master copies of the NER's siding agreements are in The National Archives at Kew. Office copies for some at least of the relevant agreements are in the Ken Hoole Study Centre, catalogue numbers JFM7341/1 to /14.

(11) TNA RAIL 527/74. NER Traffic Committee Minute 19824 of 3 March 1898.

(12) TNA MT 6/162/4. Inspection Report. For the removal of the signals and switches: TNA RAIL 667/95. Officers' Meeting Minutes, 1874 - 1879, page 187.

(13) TNA RAIL 667/31. S&DR Board Minutes, 23 April and 28 May 1830.

(14) Traffic statistics throughout this book from: RAIL 527/1166 Traffic Details for all NER Stations, 1885 - 1896; RAIL 527/1167 Traffic Details for all NER Stations, 1897 - 1907; RAIL 398/293 Station Traffic Book, 1910 - 1934; RAIL 527/2146 Station Traffic Indices, 1906-1921.

(15) See the NER's plan of Fighting Cocks Goods Station, reference number S/1/342/1 dated 17 July 1908 (NERA 1418-17-06).

(16) Details of blast furnace activity from LNER statistics and Rider, P and Owen, JG, *Blast Furnace Statistics, 1790 – 1980*, Merton Priory Press Limited, 1995.

(17) Siding Agreement between Cloke's Extension Limited and the LNER, David J Williamson Collection. For further details of the ironworks and slag processing plant, see: Mountford, CE and Holroyde, D, *The Industrial Railways & Locomotives of County Durham*, IRS, 2006. Note that in this book Middleton Iron Works and Dinsdale Moor Iron Works are described as being the same establishment; they were not, being located south and north of Fighting Cocks station respectively.

(18) Siding Agreement between Glico Petroleum Limited and the LNER, David J Williamson Collection.

(19) The S&DR had introduced Absolute Block in stages during the 1870s; in 1875, in the S&DR's annual return to the Board of Trade, it was stated that the whole route from Forcett Junction to Saltburn was now worked on the Absolute Block System.

(20) BR (NER) Drawing 50-YS-145/1 *Lingfield Lane SB, Signalling*, dated 14 April 1950, and amended May 1967 to show closure. Collection of the late CJ Woolstenholmes.

(21) Cantrell, AH, *Long Welded Rails*, Railway Gazette, Volume 71, August 1939.

(22) Depot shunter details from: Mountford, CE and Holroyde, D, *The Industrial Railways & Locomotives of County Durham*, IRS, 2006.

(23) Withdrawn steam locomotives were stored in the sidings at Fighting Cocks until they could be scrapped at North Road Works. Noted on 6 January 1959 were D49 No 62730, A5 No 69828 and J25 Nos 65655 and 65696.

(24) The singling of the former S&DR over S&D Crossing was worked up on paper in 1952: drawing 52-YS-174. The proposed interlocking was changed subsequently, and a revision to the drawing made in 1955: 55-YS-806.

(25) Hoole, K, *A Regional History of the Railways of Great Britain : Volume 4 The North East*, David & Charles, 3rd edition, 1986, page 118.

(26) BR (NER) Drawing 50-YS-145/1 *Lingfield Lane SB, Signalling*, dated 14 April 1950, and amended May 1967 to show closure. Collection of the late CJ Woolstenholmes.

(27) Closure date from a signalling diagram drawn by the late John Boyes.

(28) Information courtesy of the late Ray Goad.

(29) BR (ER) *Supplementary Notice of Signalling Alterations affecting the working of the line from Sunday 8 October 1972 between Darlington - Urlay Nook*. October 1972.

Croft Depot Branch

(30) Closure date from the notice posted by BR (North Eastern Region) at the depot in early 1964.

Forcett Railway

(31) 28 & 29 Victoria Cap. lxi. *An Act to incorporate a Company for making a Railway from the Darlington and Barnard Castle Branch of the North Eastern Railway, near Gainford, in the County of Durham, to Forcett, in the North Riding of the County of York; to authorize working and other arrangements with the North Eastern Railway Company; and for other purposes.* The Forcett Railway Company and the Forcett Limestone Company were closely associated, sharing the same Registered Office, first at 88 Northgate, Darlington, and later in Dixon Terrace. Secretary to both companies was a Barnard Castle solicitor, Thompson Richardson.

(32) The wheelbarrow, complete with silver plaque, is preserved in the Head of Steam : Darlington Railway Museum. The engraving on the plaque says that the wheelbarrow was presented to Mrs Michell, though newspaper reports state that it was Miss Michell who actually used it on the day.

(33) That the quarry company's locomotives hauled the limestone trains over North Eastern metals as far as Piercebridge – rather than simply as far as Forcett Junction – comes from Tomlinson's 1916 article in the *North Eastern*

Railway Magazine.

(34) The North Eastern's Board authorised the doubling on 21 February 1866.

(35) Information on the sidings comes from *Traffic for and from Collieries, Works, Sidings & Depots connected with the North Eastern Railway*, 1898 and *Instructions to Agents*, 1918. The dates when sidings were laid in is not known. Forcett Junction Siding is not mentioned in either the 1898 or the 1918 publications, though it is marked on the 1923 Line Diagram. It may have been provided for operational reasons rather than to serve a trader. At 8 chains 9 yards long, it was much longer than the other sidings on the line.

(36) The Census records another engine driver: Isaac Abbott, the son of Richard Abbott, who was the quarry manager. Richard's grandson, also Richard Abbott, was a clerk in the quarry office. John Elenor and his 14 year old son John W are recorded in the Census as platelayers. Wilson Elenor, who was presumably a relative, was recorded as being the station master.

(37) *Kelly's Post Office Directory . . .*, 1872.

(38) *Bulmer's History and Directory of North Yorkshire*, 1890.

(39) The warehouse is shown on the LNER's Forcett Branch Line Diagram, dated May 1923.

(40) The date 1865 comes from Holmes, PJ, *Passenger Traffic on the Stockton & Darlington Railway*. This book states that S&DR Third Class carriages for market traffic Nos 178 – 183 were built in 1864 and 1865, with No 179 being built in the latter year.

(41) See NERA Archive file NERA 1116, correspondence re working the limestone traffic.

(42) The doubling of the line Darlington (Hopetown Junction) to Piercebridge was authorised on 19 June 1867 at an estimated cost of £11,000, although the contract was not actually let till May 1869.

(43) TNA MT 6/67/10, Inspection Report.

(44) See NERA Archive file 1324-2 : *Regulations for working the line between Forcett Junction and Quarry. General Instructions*, February 1871.

(45) NERA KP Plant Collection.

(46) *Appendix A to the General Rules and Regulations, and to the Working Time Table . . . From 1 January 1898, and until further notice.*

(47) Gleave, JT. *The Teesside Iron and Steel Industry, The Geographical Journal*, May 1938.

(48) *Ibid.*

(49) Tomlinson, WW. *The Forcett Railway, North Eastern Railway Magazine*, September 1916.

(50) Information concerning the exhaustion of stone suitable for use as ballast courtesy Jim Shields.

Merrybent & Darlington Railway

(51) For further information, see Hornshaw, TR. *Copper Mining in Middleton Tyas*. North Yorkshire County Council, 1975.

(52) 29 & 30 Victoria, Cap. lxxv *An Act to incorporate a Company for making a Railway to be called "the Merrybent and Darlington Railway", and a Branch therefrom; to authorize Working and Traffic Arrangements with the North-eastern Railway Company; and for other Purposes.*

(53) GA Middlemas, Auctioneer, disposed of the contractor's plant and machinery used in the construction of the Merrybent & Darlington Railway on 7 July 1870. Items sold off from the yard at Low Coniscliffe included a tank locomotive built by Neilson of Glasgow 'little worse than new', 100 'Contractors' Earth Wagons', 130 tons of 'Contractors' Iron Rails' and a 'large Overhead Goliah Crane, with Purchases, Blocks, &c.'. See *The Darlington & Stockton Times*, 25 June 1870.

(54) 41 & 42 Victoria, Cap. xciii *An Act to provide for the winding up of the Merrybent and Darlington Railway.*

(55) 63 & 64 Victoria, Cap. clxiii *An Act to confer additional Powers upon the North Eastern Railway Company for the construction of new Railways, and other Works and the acquisition of additional lands and upon that Company and the London & North Western Railway Company in respect of Leeds New Station and for vesting in the Company the Londonderry (Seaham to Sunderland) Railway the Cawood Wistow & Selby Light Railway and the Merrybent & Darlington Railway and for other Purposes.*

(56) *Traffic for and from Collieries, Works, Sidings & Depôts connected with the North Eastern Railway*, 1898.

(57) See *The Darlington & Stockton Times*, 22 January 1870.

(58) Hoole, K. *The Stainmore Railway*, Dalesman, 1973.

(59) *Industrial Locomotives of the North Riding*. Birmingham Locomotive Club [Industrial Railway Society], 1963.

(60) See *The Northern Echo*, 29 June 2005.

(61) See *The Darlington & Stockton Times*, 16 November 1946.

(62) See *The Darlington & Stockton Times*, 28 January 1950.

(63) See Semmens, PWB, *Branch Line into Motorway. Railway Magazine*, September 1964.

Forcett Branch
Summary Distance Table (selected locations)

Zero Post : mean of points, junction with the main line.

Forcett Junction Siding	0 miles 14.35 chains
Tees Viaduct, commencement	0 miles 54.34 chains
Tees Viaduct, centre point	0 miles 56.68 chains
Tees Viaduct, termination	0 miles 59.03 chains
Lowfield Siding	1 mile 75.97 chains
Bridge No 10, 'Green Lane'	2 miles 2.33 chains
Bridge No 15, 'Tank Bridge'	3 miles 41.00 chains
Engine Shed Siding	3 miles 44.59 chains
Forcett Park Siding	3 miles 55.87 chains
Forcett Valley Junction	4 miles 35.97 chains
Gates across railway, entrance to Forcett Goods	4 miles 63.73 chains
End of Branch	4 miles 76.92 chains

Forcett Quarry Branch

Forcett Valley Junction	4 miles 35.97 chains
Forcett Valley Siding	4 miles 38.60 chains
Exchange Sidings	4 miles 48.98 chains
Coal depôt siding	4 miles 70.85 chains
Railway company boundary	4 miles 72.32 chains

Merrybent Branch
Summary Distance Table (selected locations)

Zero Post : mean of points, junction with the main line.

Siding	0 miles 5.03 chains
Exchange Siding	0 miles 5.14 chains
Coniscliffe Depôt and Siding	1 mile 25.25 chains
Bridge No 11 (Tees Bridge) commencement	2 miles 4.68 chains
Bridge No 11 (Tees Bridge) termination	2 miles 9.25 chains
Cleasby Siding	2 miles 70.24 chains
Bridge No 17 (Clow Beck)	4 miles 8.20 chains
Newton Morrell Siding	4 miles 33.62 chains
Barton Goods Station	5 miles 2.81 chains
Barton DP	5 miles 5.86 chains
Relief Siding	5 miles 52.43 chains
Railway Company boundary	5 miles 67.97 chains